Ace the SAT Essay

Ace the SAT Essay

HOW TO MASTER THE TIMED WRITING PROCESS

A Practical Guide to
the Psychology of Thinking on Your Seat

Dana L. Lebo, PhD

Zeig, Tucker & Theisen
Phoenix   Arizona

— Dedication —

To my husband, Andrew Werden; my parents, Art and Nancy Lebo; and my children, Sandra Deluzio, Alex, Jeremy, and Jacob Werden.

Copyright 2010 Dana L. Lebo

All rights reserved under International and Pan-American Copyright Conventions. No part of this book may be reproduced, stored in a retrieval system or transmitted in any form by an electronic, mechanical, photocopying, recording means or otherwise, without prior written permission of the author.

Published by
Zeig, Tucker & Theisen
3614 North 24th Street
Phoenix, AZ 85016

Manufactured in the United States of America

Contents

Introduction ix

Part I: Get Ready to T.H.I.N.K. and W.R.I.T.E.

Chapter 1: The SAT Essay 3
Chapter 2: Know your Writing Process 11
Chapter 3: Know the Writing Task 25

Part II: T.H.I.N.K. to Write

Chapter 4: *T*ransform Your Mood—Part I 39
Chapter 5: *H*op into Gear/s 47
Chapter 6: *T*ransform Your Mood—Part II 59
Chapter 7: *I*deate: *Ideas*—Gener*ate* Some! 71
Chapter 8: *N*arrate with Insight 85
Chapter 9: *K*eep your Focus 97

Part III: W.R.I.T.E. to Think

Chapter 10: *W*rite your Introduction, Body, and Conclusion 111
Chapter 11: *R*eflect on your Experience: Compelling Telling 125
Chapter 12: *I*llustrate Your Experience: Showing 137
Chapter 13: *T*ie your Ideas Together: Smooth Transitioning 157
Chapter 14: *E*ngage your Reader:
       Expressing your Voice Clearly 171

Epilogue 191
Bibliography 195

Acknowledgements

This book would not be here without the inspiration of countless high school students in *The Write Workshop* (www.bellleadership.com), my summer program for young writers. Over the years, these remarkable teenagers showed me how they could spark in each other their most powerful, honest, and insightful writing. Their energy was contagious, sparking in me the excitement and ideas to write this book.

I want to thank my husband, Andrew Werden, for his undying love and generosity, tireless patience, and unquestioning support of his family, no matter what he has on his own plate. I am grateful to my parents, Arthur and Nancy Lebo, who do whatever is needed to help us manage the challenges of each day, whether driving the kids to swim practice, proofreading this book, or folding mountains of laundry. Appreciation also goes to my daughter, Sandra Deluzio, her husband Joe, and my sons, Alex, Jeremy, and Jacob Werden for their many precious talents and gifts that enrich my life daily.

I am thankful for the support of Dr. Gerald Bell, founder of Bell Leadership Institute, and colleagues Colleen Jelley and Sharon Kolk who helped launch *The Write Workshop* in Chapel Hill, North Carolina. To the entire Bell Leadership Team I owe a depth of gratitude for teaching me each day the true meaning of leadership and providing me the opportunity to work and learn among the world's greatest Achievers.

Thanks, too, to my old friends Diane Taylor and her team at West Windsor Plainsboro Community Education for sponsoring the first few years of the *The Write Workshop* in New Jersey.

I also appreciate the suggestions of writers and teachers Carol Henderson (www.carolhenderson.com) and Linda Hobson, who believed in a book for young writers and offered their ideas and encouragement.

Finally, thanks are owed to Dr. Jeffrey Zeig and his Master Class of "frequent fliers" in New York (www.helenadrienne.com), a group of infinitely wise and exceptionally talented master therapists, highly skilled in teaching, listening, mentoring, and helping each other even through the rigors of writing and publishing. I am grateful for their continued support and friendship.

Introduction

Seeds from the Past

I eyed the clock—only ten more minutes before the final bell. A warm breeze wafted through the window, carrying a thin scent of dandelions and freshly cut grass. I heard the crack of baseball bats on the field below—hmm, warming up early. Dr. Scalera was as good as teachers get, but we had given her about all the attention high school seniors could muster on a late spring day. Freedom was minutes away. We couldn't wait to explode from our seats.

"Hold on—one last thing for this afternoon," Dr. Scalera said in response to our rustling. "I haven't finished correcting yesterday's tests but did read through your essays on *The Miracle Worker*. I want to share one of them with you."

I moaned in chorus with my peers, but secretly wished—as every student was probably wishing—that she would read my essay. Dr. Scalera's ultimate praise was to read our work aloud—no matter how embarrassed we might be in the process. To her, the humiliation of one student—real or feigned—was a small price to pay for what the class could learn by hearing a good model of prose. With the anonymous work in hand, she walked to the podium, pushed her glasses to the bridge of her nose, and cleared her throat.

As the words of the essay mingled with the fresh breeze, I leaned forward. *Who wrote this*? I wondered. It sounded new, yet vaguely familiar.

Dr. Scalera's voice rose with the force of the passage; she hurled action words at us, sensory details, metaphors of water and light. I gasped at the description of the moment when Helen Keller, from her dark world void of images and sounds, discovered she could use language to connect with others. Somehow, I felt as if I, too, were in that moment. I could see the pump where Helen knelt with her teacher. I could hear the rush of water over their hands... Suddenly, I realized that my pulses were throbbing and my cheeks were fiery hot.

"Now *that's* a conclusion," Dr. Scalera said, clutching the sides of the podium.

There was a strange silence. We remained fixed in our seats, as if the first person to move or speak would break the spell.

Finally, the kid behind me spoke. "Oh my God, someone in this *room* wrote that?"

"Yes," Dr. Scalera whispered.

I remained motionless, waiting to hear, and perhaps on some unconscious level, already knowing who had written with such power. I felt my cheeks grow even hotter. Over the rim of her glasses, Dr. Scalera was peering at me. "Nice work, Ms. Lebo," she nodded.

The bell rang and chaos broke loose.

"Good job, Lebo," a friend said and others patted me on the back. I tried to look humble. As the wave of students rushed to freedom, I embraced a curious freedom of my own. Somewhere, deep inside of me, I had found the language to express Helen Keller's awakening. I described the first moment that she communicated to her teacher by using her hands to form words. And now, I could barely move from hearing the force of my own words. *It was as if they had been written by someone else.*

So what does my story have to do with the SAT essay?

Many years later, I still marvel at the experience of what athletes call being "in the zone." That afternoon in Dr. Scalera's English class was not the first time I had entered this state, nor would it be the last. It happens sometimes when I write, paint, run, speak in front of a group, act on a stage, or even read a good book. I know that when I am in the zone, I'm performing at my best. If I had to write the SAT essay today, I would want to be in the zone.

Although we did not have the SAT writing requirement way back in the twentieth century, we did have to face similar challenges. In a room without air conditioning, we wrote our *Miracle Worker* essays in less than twenty-five minutes, responding to a prompt that was probably similar to the ones given today on the SAT.

Keep in mind, I wasn't particularly good at grammar; in fact, one teacher complained that I could "shake out commas like salt and pepper," making it hard for him to understand my ideas. I also had some traumatic experiences in which my writing did *not* flow. In those cases, I completely "blanked." My anxiety got the best of me. And among the countless essays I have written over the years are ones that would put the most persistent readers to sleep by paragraph three. Yes, I have experienced a wide range of feedback on my writing—from A +'s to D's.

Write with "insight" says the College Board

How, I wonder, would I do on the SAT essay today? To achieve a high grade, the College Board, made up of those who develop, administer, and score the exam, says you must "organize" and "develop" your ideas using "clear, appropriate examples" to support them. You must "display consistent facility in the use of language," and "demonstrate variety in your sentence structure and range of vocabulary." And to claim a "6," the highest score of all, you must "effectively and insightfully address the writing task."

Only after I began to work as a psychologist and writing teacher did I grasp what it means to write *effectively* and *insightfully*. The students who write effective essays address the writing task all right, but something more fuels their success. They achieve *insight* during the writing process. And it is this moment of insight—a special form of seeing—that enables them to write in the zone.

According to a standard dictionary, insight is "seeing with the eyes of the mind" and "directly knowing" with the wisdom of the heart. Sure, it pays to be smart—but our intellects alone do not make us good writers. Heartfelt words might help, but they are not enough to achieve an above-average score on an essay. It is when we write with our *hearts* in *mind* that we experience a unique state of being.

Like the athlete in the zone, we know intuitively what to do. We trust our body and senses to do their job—to let the words flow naturally from our insights.

The student essays that grab me the most show a natural stream of ideas and feelings. In fact, some of the genuine insights that students gain from writing about their experiences take my breath away. For example, one high school senior wrote about how she felt compelled to betray a friend's life-threatening secret to a school guidance counselor. As a result, she lost the friendship. Yet she saved her friend and concluded her essay with the realization, "My friends are more important than my friendships."

A high school junior who was suspended from school for taking drugs wrote, "Why did I do it? I wish I could say it was as simple as peer pressure. That I was a victim. But it wasn't and I wasn't. It was my choice to do it and my choice alone...when the opportunity came up that night to artificially cure my self-consciousness, at least temporarily, I took it."

These students can write powerful essays in a few minutes. They are able to reflect on their experiences in a new light because they write with their hearts in mind. By joining what they know with how they feel, their words come to life and engage the reader's interest.

My students helped me stumble upon an important but age-old discovery. We achieve insight by the same process that scientists and artists, among others, have been exploring for centuries. As a psychologist and teacher of writing, I grew increasingly aware of the common ground between two fields. Through psychology and writing, we find the words to understand the world, others, and our selves. We discover solutions to our personal problems. We get to the root of our difficulties. We reflect on life by knowing with our hearts and seeing with our minds.

The College Board appears to think along the same track. To them, insight is what distinguishes the most effective essays from the rest. If you can show your deep understanding of the topic and convey the meaning you have made out of your experience, you stand a better chance of scoring high on the essay test.

In this book, I'll share some of the lessons that psychology offers about how to write insightfully and effectively. I will also present what the writing process reveals about psychology—how writing can help you learn about your self and others. Sure, finding the right words to relate our thoughts and feelings to others might be difficult. But we are born to face this challenge. We have a voice to express the raw meaning of our own and others' experiences—what these experiences might mean to us and our readers. The voice of inner truth can emerge at any time and any place.

After all, if Helen Keller, stripped of vision and hearing in a world of darkness, could find her writer's voice, then perhaps doing so is part of what it means to be human. No other species has the ability to acquire common sense and wisdom through the accumulation of life experience. Writing sparks our inborn capacity to make our lives more meaningful. And to make our lives more meaningful, we call upon our selves to write. Like Helen Keller, we might even discover a voice that has been brewing within for a long, long time—a voice ready to explode on the page.

How this Book Will Help: A Writer's Roadmap

As you prepare for the SAT, this book will empower you to produce an above-average essay. Unlike other texts on writing or SAT preparation, this book will show you how an understanding of psychology can enhance how you write and what you say. Through the story of Jamie, a high school student who must take the writing test again after her poor performance on it the first time around, you will explore ideas and strategies to manage anxiety and create an "effective and insightful" essay. A roadmap of this journey follows.

Part One will help you to strengthen some key ingredients of successful writing: your desire to write, your command of the process, and your comfort with the task. You will learn what *you* can expect *from* the SAT writing assignment, as well as what is expected *from you* on the assignment. Through Jamie's discussions with Mrs. Flaherty, her language arts teacher, you can compare your own SAT essay-writing skills to Jamie's, and set specific goals to bring your writing performance up to Jamie's degree of mastery.

In **Part Two**, you will explore with Jamie and Mrs. Flaherty the meaning of insight and "flow"—processes that will breathe life into your SAT essay. Also, Jamie's sessions with Mr. Johnson, her school's athletic trainer and mental skills coach, will guide you in the arts of managing anxiety, tuning into your self, and writing "in the zone."

While Parts One and Two are aimed at the SAT task and improving your writing *process*, Part Three focuses on ways to enhance the *content* of your writing. The final chapters will help you to explore the use, development, and organization of examples from your experience and practice techniques to strengthen the fluidity, richness, and clarity of your writer's voice.

So whatever your present level of proficiency at writing may be, the overall aim of this book is to raise it. If you read with an open heart and mind, adapt the suggested strategies to your personal learning styles and interests, and tackle for a few minutes each day the recommended exercises at the end of each chapter—you should experience marked improvements in what and how you write.

In fact, you might gain so much confidence that you look forward to the discoveries your writing can reveal about your self. It happened to me on that warm May day in Dr. Scalera's class. May the voice of the writer within you emerge!

—*Dana L. Lebo, PhD*

Part 1

Get Ready to T.H.I.N.K. and W.R.I.T.E.

Chapter One

The SAT Essay

The Case of Kalin and Jamie

The metal band holding the eraser squashed flat between her teeth. *Oh, yuck.* Kalin dropped the pencil to her desk and began pulling eraser grit off her tongue. She had just destroyed her third writing instrument in the first five minutes of the exam—only two pencils and twenty minutes left to write an essay.

Once again, Kalin read the question—but the words refused to penetrate.

Think about the idea presented in the following proverb and the assignment below.

When one door shuts, another opens.

Assignment: For hundreds of years, famous writers from Miguel de Cervantes, 17th-century author of *Don Quixote*, to Helen Keller who wrote *The Open Door* in 1957, have referred to this proverb in their work. Is the idea expressed in this proverb as meaningful to you today? Does another door indeed open when one door shuts? Plan and write an essay in which you develop your viewpoint about this idea. Use reasons and examples from your experience, reading, studies, or observations to support your point of view.

"Huh?" Kalin sighed in frustration. Suddenly, *snap!* Her fourth pencil, which she had been clutching tightly, was now useless.

Jamie, seated behind Kalin, didn't flinch at the sound of splintering wood but continued to write feverishly. Unlike Kalin, Jamie did not have to read the essay question over and over again hoping the words would sink in. Much like a competitive sprinter who gears for the big race, Jamie knew what to expect even before she had entered the room. Already well-versed in the three different types of essay assignments that might appear on the exam, she was ready for any question the examiners could throw at her.

Jamie also knew how to put herself into a relaxed but focused state of mind and body. Being "in the zone" enabled her to perform at her peak whether playing on the sports field or writing at her desk.

Like the successful athlete, Jamie responded to her assignment with positive self-talk. "I can do this!" she thought. Seconds after reading the essay prompt, she had chosen her topic and the reasons for her choice.

"The biggest turning point for me," she said to herself, "was my parents divorce. From the moment Mom and Dad announced their separation, my family relationships changed. Hmmm. They were tense at first, but got better. I grew closer to my brother. My father cried in front of me—something he never used to do. My mother stopped treating me like the baby of the family. And when my parents found new partners, I developed even more family relationships."

Five minutes into the exam, Jamie had coached herself through a process of brainstorming and organizing the specific evidence and details to support her reasoning. By the ten-minute mark, she had developed a compelling "hook" and introduction. With more than half the time remaining, Jamie was diving into her essay's body paragraphs and writing her way towards a powerful, full-circle conclusion.

Although Jamie was seated behind her, Kalin could sense her friend's total absorption in the essay. "I hate her, " Kalin thought, feeling the pit of disappointment in her stomach and eying her own meager paragraph. She still didn't understand what the topic was. But she knew Jamie had worked hard to prepare for this test. With a sigh, Kalin decided, "I need some food. I should ask Jamie what she ate for breakfast this morning."

In the above scenario, Kalin and Jamie are having radically different test experiences. While Kalin is struggling to get started, Jamie's pen doesn't stop. She is wholly caught up in the flow of her writing and well on the road to completing a high-scoring essay within the time limit. She knows how to write with her heart in mind.

Chances are you know a student like Kalin who is sometimes crippled by test anxiety, and someone like Jamie who doesn't appear the least bit fazed by the pressure of an exam. In fact, you might find yourself identifying with Kalin or Jamie—maybe both.

Hours of Practice Make it Look Simple

Recall, for example, a time when you struggled to do something. Did you ride a two-wheel bike on the first try? Did you learn the letters of the alphabet overnight? Did you master algebra after one class? Did you make several mistakes before getting things right?

Maybe you can recall other moments when you performed your best with minimal effort. You "aced" the test. You smacked the baseball over the fence. Or you played the piano or violin like you never played before. Whatever your achievement, hours of practice certainly contributed to your performance. Those who are masters of their game usually take countless hours of effort to reach a level of mastery. They make their game look easy. But years of struggle and persistence are behind their "effortless" performance.

Jamie, too, practiced various writing skills before she could write with such ease. Like Kalin, her mind froze the first time she faced the SAT essay. She barely eked out a paragraph before the twenty-five minute time limit was up. Jamie had always considered herself a good writer—but writing effectively under time pressure was different. She wasn't used to responding to a test prompt and developing a persuasive argument in mere minutes.

Knowing that she could take the SAT over, Jamie sought advice and help from the teachers at her school. Each day, she applied the techniques they had suggested to improve her writing. A few minutes a day and Jamie could see progress.

In the next few chapters, you, too, will become acquainted with the ideas and psychological strategies that enabled Jamie to make the most of each exam minute. And like Jamie, you can adapt and apply this information to meet your own needs. A little time daily is all it takes to enhance what you write and how you write it. In short, the secret to writing a high-scoring SAT essay is a simple one: *"Practice, practice, practice!"*

Imagine You Are There

On the morning of the SAT, you will get the chance to apply the fruits of your efforts. Like Jamie, you will have the opportunity for the writer within you to emerge. You will be composing an essay. Maybe you are already familiar with the test or perhaps you are approaching it for the first time. In any case, let's review the typical SAT writing assignment.

In a nutshell, here's the task: *In the next twenty-five minutes, write about your most worthwhile experience and explain the reasons for your choice.*

Be sure to control your anxiety—for your score, if not the whole essay, will be transmitted to all the colleges of your choice. Years down the road, you may even be questioned in a job interview about your performance on this exam.

Once you have come to terms with the possibility that your entire future is on the line, and you have calmed yourself down enough to actually absorb what the question is asking you, try a little brainstorming to address it. On scratch paper, generate a few ideas from your experience. Draw from your reading or observations. Go ahead. Unleash your creative energy. Let the force be ... Okay. Don't let go *too* much. Because you must save some of your energy to organize and develop your ideas. You have yet to tie them together in a cohesive argument. So let your creative thoughts flow, but keep them in check. And keep your eye on the clock.

While you order your thoughts and your time, the College Board also expects you to demonstrate some facility and variety in your use of language, sentence structure, and vocabulary. Resist your urge to begin every sentence with "I." Show your mastery of the conventions of modern Standard English. Above all, remember to throw in some insight. For insight is the mark of a high-scoring essay. By the way, what exactly *is* insight?

As you are figuring insight out, rest assured that you are allowed to make an *occasional* grammatical error or two. Somewhere in Iowa, graders trained to quickly rate your essay according to a 1 to 6 scoring guide will keep in mind that you are only human. After all, how many sixteen-year-olds can draft the perfect essay in twenty-five minutes? But don't overdo the mistakes either. Too many errors make it hard for your graders to understand your overall argument and any insights you might have to support it.

Besides, your graders show each other a little room for error, themselves. About thirty percent of the time, the two graders assigned to an essay will disagree on the score. In that case, a third reader, maybe even a fourth will be called in to settle the conflict.

Keep in mind, too, that after two graders have added their scores for your essay, the result is combined with the raw score from the grammar portion of the SAT. It is then converted to an overall writing score on a 200-to-800 scale. By that point, your half-baked concluding sentence may be—thank goodness—lost in the sauce.

And for those of you who identified with Kalin's experience, don't forget to start writing. Because before you know it, your time will be up!

A Daunting Task

As you can see, the SAT essay requirement poses quite a challenge to the typical student. Let's admit it. The thought of writing an organized, developed, and insightful essay in twenty-five minutes can be downright intimidating even to the most proficient of writers. So those among you who are groaning and squirming in your seats, I hear you.

You might be asking, "Why do I have to take this test in the first place? What's in it for me? When can anxiety be *good*?"

The answers to these questions might help you to embrace the SAT essay challenge. All right. Maybe *embrace* is a strong word. At least you can head to the exam room knowing that the skills you developed to write a successful SAT essay are well worth the investment of your time and effort. Chances are that they will help you throughout your lifetime.

"Why do we I have to take this test? What's in it for me?"

Let's consider more fully the background and purpose for the SAT essay. After all, many experts agree that to perform a task that is forced upon you, it helps to have a firm understanding of, "What's in it for me?"

In response to, "What's in it for me?" Richard Atkinson, the psychologist whose views on standardized testing once landed him on the cover of *Time* magazine in 2001, said that translating your thoughts to writing is a skill that is "critical for success in college and beyond." Although educators across the country have long considered writing as fundamental as reading and arithmetic, the SAT I at the turn of the 21st century failed to include a basic test of written human expression.

This shortcoming is one of the reasons that Dr. Atkinson, also President of the University of California (UC) system, recommended doing away with the SAT I as an admissions requirement for the thousands of students seeking entry to UC schools. At a 2001 meeting of the American Council on Education, Dr. Atkinson explained the basis for his decision. For years, he had been concerned that the SAT I was limited in its ability to predict students' success in college. His fears were well grounded.

One day, while observing a class of middle-school students memorizing verbal analogies—"Untruthful is to mendaciousness as circumspect is to caution"—Dr. Atkinson was gripped by the absurdity of the situation. Rather than developing their skills at reading, writing or critical thinking, these students were spending precious class time developing their skills at taking the SAT. Teachers were under pressure to "teach to the test"—not to teach what students really needed to know to prepare for college-level work.

Numerous critics joined Dr. Atkinson in his arguments to abandon the SAT I. Finally, in the summer of 2002, the College Board announced its plans to revamp the exam. Thanks to the addition of the essay requirement, more schools will focus on helping students to become better writers.

So now instead of forcing yourself to study word associations, you can relax and devote your time to developing a thesis statement and paragraphs. Yet even the most skeptical students would agree that the ability to express your thoughts on paper has a broader, more lasting impact on your life than the ability to make verbal analogies. And even skeptics might admit that what you gain from writing effectively is more than just a score on a college entrance exam. A host of psychological skills are cultivated as you write—skills that time and time again prove valuable both within and beyond the school environment.

Just what are these psychological skills that turn anxiety into a positive force, help you write a successful SAT essay—and help you succeed in other areas of life? They include the useful talent of thinking on your feet—or seat.

The Psychology of Thinking on Your Seat

How many times in your life have you been called upon to make a decision and defend it on the spot? As an adult, I face such situations daily, if not hourly. From convincing my husband of the safest route to drive our children to school on an icy morning, to defending my use of stuffed animals in a writing workshop—I am constantly challenged to think on the fly. As a teenager, you, too, may frequently find yourself justifying your opinions or actions. Your friend asks, "How can you like that boring movie?" Or your parent questions, "You want to pierce your *what*?" Or, someone confronts you: "What on *earth* has gotten into you?"

As these questions suggest, thinking on your seat may boil down to your ability to defend at that moment the choices you make. Writing is but one tool of reflection—in response to some cue, you summon or gather, you sort through, then draw meaning from your experience; you find the right language to articulate what you think. In the words of Dr. Atkinson, you "translate your thoughts" to written form.

Writing the SAT essay calls upon your capacity to think on your seat. You are asked to reflect upon the prompt, and with heart in mind to produce an effective response almost immediately. Our ancestors did it. When the saber-toothed tiger roared outside their caves, they instinctively rose on the balls of their feet and made the decision to fight or take flight. Although the SAT essay isn't a life-or-death situation, you, too, must make a speedy choice about the way to go. Then, you must defend your choice.

Thinking on your seat is what it takes to respond to questions like,

"What is the most worthwhile moment of your life and why?"

"Do you agree that every cloud has a silver lining?" or,

"Is it possible to teach an old dog new tricks?"

Like your ancestors, you may decide that a clear-cut choice is not that easy to make. Depending on the situation, fighting *and* fleeing in differing degrees may be the best response.

Whatever stand (or seat) you choose to take in response to the SAT writing prompt—no one will judge whether you are right or wrong. What matters is your ability to support your position with convincing reasons and minimal time to make your points. You won't have the chance to search for information at the library or on the Web. You must derive a rationale for your choice from what you already know—your own experience, readings or observations of the world.

Keep in mind, when our ancestors decided to fight, flee, or a combination of both—the choice itself was not as important as how *well* they performed in that choice. How hard they fought, how fast they fled, or how cunningly they outwitted the tiger was what determined their survival. Making the choice, then, is only a fraction of the task. Convincing your reader of the sense behind your choice is the heart of the essay challenge.

And in this process, you may even find that you are changing what you thought you knew. After all, how your mind and body respond to a question or problem is unique; no one else can have quite the same combination of thoughts and sensations that you experience. Writing then, becomes a process of discovery and what some psychologists call "knowledge transformation." As you ponder your ideas and the words to express them, they may connect and combine in novel ways, creating broader perspectives and deeper insights.

For example, you might start out with the conviction that you can't teach an old dog new tricks, but as you recall your surprise when your grandfather IM'd you, or when your mother created a really popular blog on blogspot.com, you start to realize that maybe old dogs can learn new tricks after all. Similarly, our ancestors, no matter how set in their ways, still discovered innovative ways to fight, flee and flourish.

As you sharpen your essay composition skills, you will explore how they can lead to success in other areas of your life. For example, achieving insight through writing is a sign of your openness and ability to learn from experience—traits that will serve you well in your school, work and family. In fact, college admissions officers welcome your capacity for continuous learning. This is a major quality they seek in candidates for their freshman class. What's more, your ability to connect with and influence others through writing may call upon some of the same leadership skills that enable you to negotiate conflict, reach a team decision, or motivate others to action—behaviors that are highly valued in the workplace. And managing your anxiety in ways that help rather than hinder your writing is similar to the work of athletes, creative artists, and any human being who must perform under stress. Spending the time, then, to practice the art of essay writing is an investment that leads to long-term results—well beyond your achieving a high score on the SAT.

Chapter Two

Know your Writing Process

Six months before acing the SAT essay, Jamie was still recovering from her first disappointing attempt to write under time pressure. She realized she had to do *some*thing to improve her performance. So she asked for help from the one person she knew could make the difference.

"Of course I'll work with you!" Mrs. Flaherty, Jamie's ninth-grade Language Arts teacher, seemed surprised that Jamie would think otherwise.

Jamie sighed in relief. "I—I know I wasn't always the easiest student, but I've calmed down a lot in the past two years," she assured her former teacher.

Mrs. Flaherty's smile disappeared quickly. She looked straight into Jamie's eyes. "I remember that things were a bit difficult for you that year. You have come a long way since then."

Jamie preferred to forget her freshman year—all of it, that is, except Mrs. Flaherty's class. Ninth grade had been Jamie's "Year of the Tornado." Her parents must have decided that adjusting to high school wasn't enough of a challenge for her. So they hit her with their divorce.

Jamie took the blow hard. Just like Dorothy in *The Wizard of Oz*, she felt like she had awakened from a bad dream about a storm, and she longed to have her home as she had known it back again. While she struggled to make sense of her new reality, Mrs. Flaherty set the stage for Jamie to experience a personal Land of Oz, complete with a yellow brick road and an odd assortment of fellow classmates and literary characters who were also looking for a place they could call home.

Jamie remembered how she felt once she walked through Mrs. Flaherty's door. She was dazzled by a brilliance that was missing from her family life. Why was it that in L.A. class she noticed colors, and at her Mom's and Dad's, just like Kansas in the Wizard of Oz, the world seemed to be in black and white?

In spite of her sense of wonderment, or maybe because of it, Jamie gave Mrs. Flaherty a hard time. In the beginning of the year, Jamie came late to class. She hid at a desk in the back of the room. But she did not allow herself to become invisible. She was bristling with so much anger that she took delight in hurling a sarcastic reply each time Mrs. Flaherty asked a question.

Yet Mrs. Flaherty remained undaunted. She somehow managed to find something redeeming in the most caustic of Jamie's remarks and would often say, in her respectful tone, "That's an interesting view, Jamie. One I hadn't thought of before. Thank you for broadening my perspective!" And no matter how meager Jamie's writing, Mrs. Flaherty always managed to find one sentence that she deemed *"beautifully written!"* She would then ask just the right question that compelled Jamie to *"expand"* her thoughts.

Gradually, Jamie's sarcastic remarks turned to witty ones. Maybe her weekly trips to the guidance counselor for "anger management" were paying off, even though all she did was sit and glower at poor Mr. Hatchett for half an hour straight. Nevertheless, the class began to laugh instead of cringe at Jamie's unique brand of humor. Mrs. Flaherty often laughed the hardest.

Looking back, Jamie realized the role that Mrs. Flaherty had played in her life. At a time when her self-doubt was climbing to staggering heights, she needed to know that she wasn't alone or crazy. She needed someone who could not only tolerate her anger, but also help her to see behind it, to see what it meant. Mrs. Flaherty offered the support, validation, and insights Jamie was seeking. Each week, the teacher seemed to know exactly what book to hand her student—as though she could read Jamie's mind and worries. Jamie found solace in the stories, poems and plays about people who were struggling to overcome adversity, as she was. *The Color Purple, The Scarlet Letter, The Big Wave, Leaving Home, how I live now, Stranger in a Strange Land, Romeo and Juliette* were just a few of the titles she remembered.

Through the language arts, Mrs. Flaherty found ways to unlock what Jamie was holding deep inside—what was waiting to be expressed. Without this outlet, Jamie was sure she would have burst. By the end of the ninth grade, Mrs. Flaherty had provided for Jamie what Glinda, the Good Witch of the North, offered Dorothy in the Land of Oz: the opportunity to believe in herself and find her own way back home.

Now two years later, Jamie once again found herself swimming in self-doubt. She felt the familiar pull towards Mrs. Flaherty's class. When she explained to her former teacher about her miserable experience on the SAT essay, Mrs. Flaherty didn't look the least bit surprised.

"You aren't the first student to come to me with this concern, Jamie. Nor will you be the last. In fact, I'm putting together an after-school SAT essay prep program for next fall. You can help me to try it out in advance, test it. I want to see if it works! Would you be willing?"

Jamie wasn't sure how she could be the one to help Mrs. Flaherty, but she figured she owed her teacher something for putting up with her anger for a whole year. "If you really think I can help you," she replied. Besides, she was glad for any excuse to spend time with the teacher who could make even the scariest of emotional roller coasters into a bearable ride.

"First, Jamie, I'll need to get a sense of *how* you write."

"*How* I write?" asked Jamie, not quite understanding what Mrs. Flaherty meant. "You've seen my writing. I don't know if it has changed much since the ninth grade."

"I don't mean *what* you write. I already know that you have interesting ideas. I mean *how* you write. In twenty-five minutes, *what* you write is going to be affected by *how* you write."

"Oh." Jamie's response was as hollow as her grasp of Mrs. Flaherty's explanation.

"Okay. Think of the last time you were asked to write an essay, paper or some other kind of composition. Can you recall the *process* of your writing? What was going on inside your head at the time? What you did automatically? What was a struggle for you? The greater your awareness of what you *do* when you write, the more you can jump start and streamline your process of writing a good essay in twenty-five minutes, and the less you will spend precious time figuring out how to get started."

Jamie shook her head. All she could remember was the panic she felt during the SAT essay. Her mind had gone blank.

Mrs. Flaherty's voice softened at her student's look of frustration. "If you have not given extensive thought to what you actually *do* when you write, Jamie—join the club. After all, quite a few people out there have been asking the same questions for years. In fact, about a quarter of a century ago at Carnegie Mellon University, a psychology professor named John Hayes and an English professor named Linda Flower thought that if they could pinpoint what people *do* when they write, perhaps they could help them to be better writers. Think about it for a second. How would you attempt to figure out what happens when someone is writing?"

Jamie pondered for a moment. "Since I can't read minds, I would have to stop the person every couple of seconds and ask, 'What did you just think about right now? What did you tell yourself to do while you were writing?' But if I kept stopping the poor person, I would interrupt what he or she is writing!"

"You're right, Jamie. For that reason, I don't think we can ever fully know what is happening while someone is writing. You're bringing up a problem that scientists have been struggling with for centuries. That is, if we observe something to understand how it happens, does our observing change what would normally take place?

"But we have to start somewhere if we're going to try to understand and build a model for the writing process. In 1981, Hayes and Flower wrote an article called *The Cognitive Process Theory of Writing*. To come up with such a theory, they had to observe numerous writers, some who were beginners and some who were experts. These writers were presented with the awkward challenge of thinking aloud about their writing process as they wrote."

Mrs. Flaherty looked as if she had experienced a sudden revelation. "Hey, why not try it yourself? Why not put yourself in the shoes of a beginning writer who is asked to comment on her writing process?"

Jamie felt slightly taken aback. A *beginning* writer? She had to remind herself that if she was an expert, she wouldn't be asking Mrs. Flaherty for help in the first place. She wouldn't have blanked on the SAT. "Okay," Jamie said guardedly. "So you mean I have to write an essay and tell you about my writing process while I am writing?"

"How about we make it a little easier. Instead of writing something right now, imagine that over the last couple of weeks, you have written not just one, but several essays or papers—both in-class and homework assignments. Pick one of these writing experiences, and try to picture yourself during the actual writing process."

Humoring Mrs. Flaherty, Jamie closed her eyes and furrowed her brows. She did her best to summon the scene in her mind's eye.

"Where do you see yourself? Are you facing your computer monitor? Seated at a desk? Sprawled on the floor? Or maybe in front of the TV set? Are you by yourself, or with other people?"

Jamie giggled. "The cafeteria. I'm sitting at a table with my friends trying to write my paper on the images of depression in one of Robert Frost's poems. The computer lab wasn't open yet, and I had to write instead of type."

"Good! Now try to recall what is going on inside your head as you look at that piece of paper before you." Mrs. Flaherty paused, then continued to speak at a slow, relaxed pace. "What are you telling yourself to do? Do you tell yourself to come up with some kind of plan for writing, or, do you merely put pen to paper and write? Perhaps you take a few minutes to think before you write, or you write for a few minutes and then stop, read it over, and think? Maybe you do both: you go back and forth between thinking and writing, writing and thinking. What goes on as you compose each sentence? What happens as you switch to a new paragraph? As you draw what you are writing to an end? Take a couple of minutes to mentally note some of the things that you remember thinking, feeling, and doing during the process."

Jamie wondered if she should divulge her most recent experience. She barely completed her paper on Frost's imagery by the deadline, rushing to finish her work during the study hall before class. Jamie's friend Kalin had brought in a box of Munchkin donut holes to celebrate her birthday with their group of study hall friends. For some reason the study hall monitor was absent, and they capitalized on the opportunity to have a Munchkin fight. Jamie remembered her unsuccessful attempts to clean the powdered sugar and jelly off her paper's title while mini Dunkin' Donuts whizzed overhead. Did she even *have* a writing process?

Out of respect for Mrs. Flaherty, Jamie forced herself to scribble a couple of thoughts on the paper: *I try to put the essay question into my own words. I brainstorm ideas. I think of my thesis. I write an outline.* Jamie knew that she was writing what Mrs. Flaherty would want to hear. She listed a few of the unrealistic techniques that her English teachers had tried to drill into her over the years. But did she ever take the time to create a web? Did she believe it was useful to fill a page with words, draw bubbles around the words and lines between the bubbles? Did she ever put together an outline before she wrote the actual essay or paper? Instead, when a teacher assigned an outline with a paper, Jamie wrote hers *after* she finished the paper. Could she admit the real truth even though it was the opposite of what Mrs. Flaherty would want to hear? Jamie's writing process was as messy and chaotic as the Munchkin fight. She felt like a fraud.

Mrs. Flaherty's voice broke into her thoughts. "After you have had a chance to reflect on your writing process, take a look at this questionnaire and response sheet. Although it applies to writing a timed essay, you can think back to the experience in the cafeteria."

Jamie gulped as Mrs. Flaherty handed her another paper. Maybe she should think of some other, less harried moments of writing. She skimmed the instructions about rating her essay-writing experience:

YOUR WRITING PROCESS

Read over the list of actions below and on a scale of 1 to 5—1 being not at all *and 5 being* all the time—*check the number on the Response Sheet that best describes your own experience of writing an essay.*

"Be honest." Mrs. Flaherty encouraged her. "After all, no one has to see your answers but you, and for your own sake, you want as accurate a picture of your writing process as possible."

"Should I do it right now?"

"Well," Mrs. Flaherty thought for a moment. "Take it home and complete it tonight, Jamie. We can meet again tomorrow at the same time, and review what your responses say about your writing process."

That evening, Jamie checked on her Response Sheet how much the statements on the following pages applied to her experience. (Find out about *your* writing process. Answer the questions #1 through #38 by filling in your own Response Sheet on page 19.

16 Part 1

YOUR WRITING PROCESS

Read over the list of actions below and on a scale of 1 to 5—1 being not at all *and 5 being* all the time—*check the number on the Response Sheet (see page 19) that best describes your own experience of writing an essay.*

1. I have a hard time getting started.

2. I easily clear my mind and concentrate on the writing task.

3. I try to understand the question or writing assignment by putting it into my own words.

4. I am easily overwhelmed by the writing task.

5. I take some time to think about what I know and/or what I have experienced to help me address the question or writing assignment.

6. I do some brainstorming about the topic before I write.

7. I feel that I know the types of essay assignments to expect on the SAT even before I see the test.

8. I make an outline or some kind of plan about what to write.

9. I just start writing without thinking about or jotting any ideas down beforehand.

10. I have a strategy for writing essays that works.

11. I make sure to start my essay with a "hook," e.g., a quotation, anecdote, image, question, metaphor or some interesting statement to grab my reader's attention.

12. I take the time to come up with a specific thesis statement or driving argument for my essay.

13. I make sure to write a topic sentence to capture the main idea for each essay paragraph.

14. I am certain that my topic sentence/main idea in each paragraph is clearly related to my thesis statement or central argument.

15. I organize my paragraphs in a way that is easy for the reader to follow.

16. I use a variety of transitions to link the paragraphs of my essay and the ideas within them.

17. I support each main idea of my essay with clear, interesting, and specific details,

e.g., explanations, elaborations, comparisons, contrasts, illustrations, sensory description, facts, observations, etc.

18. I conclude my essay with a strong statement, question, quotation, vivid image, warning, call to action, or some other way to leave a lasting impression on the reader.

19. I try to vary the length of my paragraphs and sentences.

20. I have a hard time finding just the right words to express my ideas.

21. I understand what I want to say in my essay, but I have a hard time coming up with the language to say it.

22. I notice that my sentences tend to be awkwardly worded.

23. Putting a sentence together correctly is difficult for me to do.

24. I sense some of my paragraphs or sentences are so long that they might lose the reader.

25. People have a hard time understanding what I have written because of my mistakes in grammar or language.

26. When I write the essay, I tend to get off topic.

27. When I am done with my essay, I feel that I haven't really answered the question or addressed the assignment.

28. I have a difficult time coming up with enough specific details to support each idea.

29. Writing bores me.

30. I really get into what I am writing.

31. When I write, I feel a connection with the reader.

32. When I write, time seems to disappear.

33. I am easily distracted when I write.

34. I believe that the reader can learn something from my essay.

35. I reach a deeper level of understanding through my writing.

36. I check to make sure that all the sentences in each paragraph are clearly related to the topic sentence/main idea of that paragraph.

37. I proofread, edit or revise my writing before handing it in.

38. When I am finished writing my essay, I prefer to leave it alone rather than to go back and make changes.

Know Your Writing Process

Response Sheet

Put a check in the box corresponding to the number of each of your responses to questions #1 through #38.

	1 Not at all	2 Rarely	3 Sometimes	4 Frequently	5 All of the time
Collecting Information/ Grasping Your Ideas 1 *					
2					
3					
4 *					
5					
6					
7					
Planning 8					
9 *					
10					
Translating Ideas/Plans into Writing 11					
12					
13					
14					
15					
16					
17					
18					
19					
20 *					
21 *					
22 *					
23 *					
24 *					
25 *					
26 *					
27 *					
28 *					
29 *					
30					
31					
32					
33 *					
34					
35					
Reviewing					
36					
37					
38 *					

How Does your Writing Process Measure Up?

"I answered all the questions," Jamie announced to Mrs. Flaherty the next afternoon. Her teacher was busily cleaning the chalkboard—one of the few remaining chalkboards in the entire school district, if not the entire state. Mrs. Flaherty was famous for her refusal to replace her chalkboard with the latest in whiteboard technology. The editor of the school newspaper captured Mrs. Flaherty's views on the subject with the headline: *Teacher Bored by the Whiteboard.*

"I need to hear my words click, smell the lime dust, and feel the tip of my chalk dissolve against the wall of slate," Mrs. Flaherty explained. "I need to use my senses to write. Whiteboards don't afford me such opportunity. In fact, the markers' odors just give me a headache."

Mrs. Flaherty made a few final strokes with the eraser, as if she were putting the finishing touches on a painting. "Well," she said, turning to Jamie, "Let's see what you found out about your writing process."

"Some of these questions seem to be more about what I write than the actual process." Jamie commented while sinking into a front-row seat. She rooted in her bag for the assessment and response sheet.

"That's true," Mrs. Flaherty agreed, brushing the chalk dust from her hands. "I wanted to see the extent to which you have a mental checklist in your head while you are writing your essay. In other words, as you are writing, do you automatically set goals for yourself to include a thesis statement, a topic sentence in each paragraph, adequate details to support each idea, and so on? Sounds like a long checklist, but these are the basics of an effectively written essay—something that we will talk about at greater length down the road. For now, though, to what extent *do* you check—while you are writing—that these ingredients are in your essay? The more this checklist is ingrained in your mind, the more it is an automatic part of your writing process. Why don't we take a closer look at your writing process by marking on your Response Sheet your strengths and areas of improvement." She handed Jamie a red pen.

"To do this, go back to the numbers that have a little asterisk after them, and circle each check that corresponds to a 3, 4 and 5. Once you are finished, go back to the numbers with*out* the little *, and circle each check that corresponds to a 1, 2 or 3."

Jamie followed Mrs. Flaherty's instructions.

Mrs. Flaherty continued her explanation after Jamie completed her circling. "What you are doing is picking out those activities within your overall writing process that could be improved with practice. You are also pinpointing what you do well at each stage of the writing process and what needs work. Those statements that correspond to the rows with a red circle represent what can be developed in your writing process. And then those rows without a red-circled check correspond to statements of your strengths or aspects of the writing process that are not necessarily a concern for you."

Jamie looked at her score sheet and noticed that she had red circles in each section. She shuddered. "It looks like I need a lot of practice. Well, hold on. I'm good at writing topic sentences! And I don't think that writing is boring!" She smiled meekly.

"This is a tool only, Jamie," Mrs. Flaherty reassured her. "It is not the definitive statement on your writing. But it will help me to target the areas we need to work on over the next few weeks."

"What does each of these four categories mean?" Jamie pointed to the boldly printed labels, ***Collecting Information, Planning, Translating, and Reviewing.*** "Are these the stages of the writing process?"

"You're right! These are the same categories that were identified by Hayes and Flower during their study. They found that expert writers, in comparison to novice or beginning writers, more consistently engaged in four strategies: 1) **collecting information** by pulling together ideas from various sources such as the media, books, and actual experience; 2) **planning** what to say; in other words, forming ideas and organizing them, as well as establishing goals for their writing; 3) **translating** those plans into writing by finding the words to express each idea; and 4) **reviewing** the plans or writing as it evolves, and continuously evaluating what has been written for possible errors."

"But my writing process is a lot messier then this, Mrs. Flaherty." Again, the image of flying donuts flashed in Jamie's mind. "I might do some of these things, like planning or reviewing what I write—but not in any particular order."

"That is precisely what Hayes and Flower realized. These parts of the writing process didn't happen in any specific pattern. A writer could engage in more than one aspect of the writing process at the same time, and one aspect could trigger another aspect of it. For example, I could *collect information* and *translate* my thoughts while I *plan* my essay, and my *reviewing* could lead to further *translating* and *planning*. According to Hayes and Flower, these four elements of the writing process appeared to influence each other. Today, we say that writing is a *recursive* process. Planning could lead to translating and reviewing, and translating or reviewing could lead back to planning again. In other words, the actual writing process might be quite chaotic!"

Jamie started to think that Mrs. Flaherty was getting a little too academic in her explanation. The only word to which she could relate was *chaotic*, which caused her to remember the images of the messy Munchkin donut fight. Her teacher must have read Jamie's mind, because she suddenly halted the lecture.

"So, Jamie, you may wonder, 'How does this process—the Hayes and Flower model—apply to a timed-writing task like the one I'll face on the SAT?'"

Jamie nodded in relief.

"To answer this question, I have asked the students in my classes to describe their writing processes after they have just completed a twenty-five minute SAT-like essay assignment. Drawing from what they can remember, a few explain that at first, they have to brainstorm or quickly sort through their knowledge and experience to find an example that relates to the essay question. This is a process similar to *collecting information*—except they are gathering ideas to address the question from their memories rather than from external sources of information such as the library or Internet."

Jamie could recall herself on that fateful day, SAT prompt in front of her. Her brain completely shut down. So much for her capacity to come up with ideas under time constraints.

Mrs. Flaherty went on. "About half of my students report that they "just write"—or immediately *translate* their thoughts into writing. On the other hand, the remaining half claim that they spend the first couple of minutes *planning* or outlining what to write before they start the actual essay. A small handful of students say that they have the time to 'read over,'or *review* their work by spending the final seconds of the test checking grammar, spelling or vocabulary."

Jamie knew that she was not the best planner or reviewer either. How, then, did she manage to write all these years if she skipped over entire stages of the process?

"According to my students, true to the Hayes and Flower model, even a timed-essay assignment seems to involve elements of collecting information—or gathering ideas from memory—and planning, translating and reviewing." Mrs. Flaherty seemed triumphant in her conclusion.

Jamie was uncomfortable with Mrs. Flaherty's enthusiasm. She realized that she had fallen into the mode of cutting corners when it came to writing. She was leaving out at least half of what the expert writers did to write effectively.

"You know, Jamie, Hayes and Flowers' explanation of the writing process has not changed much over the years; in fact, many educational experts have used it to guide their explorations of the most effective ways to enhance writing performance. Now that you have a clearer picture of your own writing process, you can use the ideas that we're going to talk about to reinforce what may already be working for you, or to strengthen your skills in particular areas of writing. Why not pick one of these areas in which you can strengthen your skills and we'll talk about how to do that next session."

Jamie looked again at all the red circles on her paper. "Okay," she sighed. This was going to be more work than she thought. "How about we start with the first one—collecting information. That sounds doable."

"Great! I'll see you next week! In the meantime, Jamie, one step you can take between now and then to better understand the kind of information you will be asked to collect or recall for your SAT essay is this: visit the College Board website, at ***www.collegeboard.com***. In fact, you should visit this website on a regular basis during the weeks leading up to the exam date. This way, you can read about the latest explanations and samples of the types of essay assignments that are likely to appear on the SAT."

Jamie realized that she was already familiar with the website—she had visited it to register for previous SAT's and to try some sample test questions.

"One more thing," said Mrs. Flaherty. "Take another look at your response sheet and the statements corresponding to the red-circled letters. While our discussion of the writing process is still fresh in your mind, this sheet can serve as a marker of those specific areas of collecting information, planning, translating, and reviewing that we can work on together.

"Thanks, Mrs. Flaherty." Jamie took the sheet and slid it inside her notebook. She sighed loudly. This time though, the rush of breath that escaped her lips was filled with resolve instead of resentment. She had trusted her teacher before; she would again have to trust that Mrs. Flaherty knew what she was doing.

Chapter Three

Know the Writing Task

Jamie sat at her desk, staring at the computer screen. How, she wondered, could she "collect information"—a vital aspect of the writing process, Mrs. Flaherty had said. In the SAT test room, she would not have access to the Internet, books, or the media—the places where she usually went to find information.

According to Mrs. Flaherty, though, she could have prior knowledge about the *types* of essay questions and instructions that would appear on the SAT, and the kinds of experiences she could write about. If she learned from the College Board what to expect on the test, she would have a better sense of the information she could use in her response. She could walk into the exam room with the confidence that she had this information inside her. At least, she hoped so.

Visit the College Board Website

Jamie typed **www.CollegeBoard.com** into her browser. She quickly followed the links to the SAT essay, and to her surprise, discovered that the SAT essay "question" really wasn't a question at all. Rather, students were instructed to develop an argument in response to either

1) a statement,
2) contrasting statements, or
3) an incomplete statement.

To get a better feel for the types of arguments she might be challenged to write, Jamie devoured every essay assignment she could find on the College Board website. She was glad that at the start of their next meeting, Mrs. Flaherty immediately handed her a packet of more examples.

"Jamie, remember how I told you that working with you would help me prepare some materials for future students who need help on the essay? Well, I put together some explanations and illustrations of each essay type in this little handout, based on the many examples I've collected over the years. What do you think?"

Jamie read over the following:

Types of SAT Essay Assignments

Type I: Statement

In this type of essay assignment, you are presented with a statement or a specific point of view. YOUR TASK IS TO RESPOND TO THIS STATEMENT AND PRESENT REASONS FOR YOUR RESPONSE.

Example One:

Charles Dickens began his novel, *A Tale of Two Cities*, with the line, "*It was the best of times, it was the worst of times…*" Although written in the 1800's, many Dickens' readers claim that this statement is still relevant today. In an essay, **show whether you agree or disagree with the application of Dickens's 19th Century observation to the present century.** *To support your argument, use an example or examples from history, current events, science and technology, politics, literature, the arts, or your personal experience.*

Example Two:

An old proverb says, "You can't teach an old dog new tricks."

Write an essay in which you **challenge, defend or qualify what is suggested** *in this proverb.* **To support your view, use an example or examples from history, politics, science and technology, literature, the arts, current events, or your experience or observation.**

Example Three:

It is often said that **from pain comes growth**. To put it another way, **suffering builds character. Using examples from your studies, reading, observation or experience, show** in an essay **how** a person grew stronger through pain or suffering.

Type II: Two Contrasting Statements

In this type of essay assignment, you are presented with two contrasting statements. YOUR TASK IS TO CHOOSE THE STATEMENT THAT MORE CLOSELY REFLECTS YOUR VIEW AND TO EXPLAIN YOUR CHOICE.

Example One:
   1. *Losing makes you.*
   2. *Losing breaks you.*

The first statement suggests that losing can be a defining opportunity for self-growth and the second suggests it can be a debilitating experience. Choose the statement that more closely reflects your view. Then, in an essay, **provide the reasons for your choice. Use an example or examples from science and technology, history, politics, sports, literature, the arts, current events, or your personal experience to support your view.**

Example Two:
Paul Tillich, a twentieth-century theologian, points out that our language wisely contains two words—loneliness and solitude—to express the different sides of being alone. Tillich explains that loneliness *is used to express the painful side of being alone, while* solitude *is used to express the glorious side of being alone. In an essay*, **comment on the side of being alone—the pain of loneliness or the glory of solitude —that more closely reflects your view. Use an example or examples from your reading, studies, observation, or experience.**

Example Three:
Opposites attract.
Birds of a feather flock together.
Consider the two contrasting statements above. Select the one that more closely reflects your view. Then **write an essay that explains your choice. To support your view, use an example or examples from history, literature, the arts, current events, politics, science and technology, your experience or observation.**

Type III: Incomplete Statement

You are presented with an incomplete statement, and YOUR TASK IS FIRST, TO CHOOSE THE WORD OR PHRASE THAT MOST SUITABLY COMPLETES THE STATEMENT AND SECOND, TO EXPLAIN YOUR CHOICE.

Example One:
Mohandis Gandhi once said that, "A 'No' uttered from deepest conviction is better and greater than a 'Yes' merely uttered to please, or what is worse, to avoid trouble." In my own experience or observations, one such "No" was uttered when _____ _____.
Complete the sentence above with an appropriate phrase and then **explain** *in an essay* **how** *that "No" was better and greater than a "Yes."*

Example Two:
Consider the statement below. Then write your essay as instructed.
"I have experienced a number of influential teachers in my life, but the most influential of all was (or is) _____.
Assignment: Write an essay completing this statement. **Be sure to explain the reasons for your choice.**

Example Three:
Michel de Montaigne, the French essayist, wrote that, "There are some defeats more triumphant than victories." Although this comment was made over four centuries ago, it still applies to the present period. An example of one such defeat was (or is) _____.
Choose a suitable phrase to complete the above statement. In an essay, **show how** *this particular defeat was/is more triumphant than victory, and* **explain the reasons for your choice.**

Example Four:
   Hitherto _____ ; henceforth, things will be quite different. Hitherto and henceforth (transitional expressions of Old English origin) are rarely used today in either written or spoken form. The word hitherto means until this time or up to now; the term henceforth means from this time forward or from now on. In combination, these terms may signal a change or turning point in events. Complete the above sentence with a suitable phrase for something that has been happening up to this point, but will be quite different from now on. In an essay, describe this change and explain what will be different.

What to Expect on the SAT Essay: Some Common Themes

After reading the entire handout, Jamie looked up at Mrs. Flaherty who was grading papers at her desk.

"Can you pick out what you are asked to do in each of those assignments, Jamie? Do you notice what they have in common?" Mrs. Flaherty pushed aside her papers and to Jamie's surprise, opened a little notebook as if she were a reporter about to conduct an interview.

"After reading enough of these, even *I* can see a pattern," Jamie smiled at her teacher. "They all seem to ask me to argue for or against some kind of statement—either a complete statement or one that I, myself, have to fill in."

Mrs. Flaherty nodded while she scribbled on her pad.

"And the statements usually have to do with something famous someone once said, or with some literary, historical or political idea...."

"Yep." Mrs. Flaherty seemed delighted with Jamie's response. "If you can show your competency at developing an argument in support of—or against—the statement that is presented in the assignment, you are on the road to writing an effective essay. In a nutshell, Jamie, you are asked to do three things."

Jamie quickly opened her own notebook—ready to capture Mrs. Flaherty's summary of what was expected of her on the exam.

"First," Mrs. Flaherty observed, "The statements in all three types of essay assignments are quotations, proverbs, philosophies, etc., that suggest universal themes, ideas, or experiences to which we can usually relate in some way. For example, the expression *"A 'no' uttered from deepest conviction"* may suggest to some the universal theme of non-conformity or resistance to authority. Perhaps, at some point in your life, you stood up for something that was important to you, or you read about or observed others fighting for their beliefs."

Jamie thought about the debates that they were having in her social studies class. Two days ago, she had to present an argument in support of lowering the legal age in her state for drinking alcohol from twenty-one to eighteen. Although her argument won applause, her opponent's argument to keep the minimum age at twenty-one was ultimately more convincing—especially after he quoted some sobering statistics about teenage drinking and driving. After the debate, the teacher asked the class how many of them knew or had heard of a teenager who had died at the wheel while under the influence of alcohol. The entire class raised their hands. Everyone could relate to the opponent's viewpoint.

Jamie wrote in her notebook:

1. Identify the Universal Theme or Idea

"Also," Mrs. Flaherty continued, "the contrasting statements *opposites attract* and *birds of a feather flock together* may suggest either the experience of joining with people who are different from us or bonding with those who are like us in some way.

Mrs. Flaherty chuckled. "I do a little icebreaker activity at the beginning of the school year to illustrate this point. I ask my students first to share something with the class that no one else knows about them—something they feel good about—like the time they won the hula hoop contest in first grade. I then ask them to imagine they have to invite one person in class to go to lunch with them—on the basis of the information they just learned about each other. They end up picking someone who can teach them a new thing—like how to hang glide."

"Or, they select a fellow student who can complement their strengths in some way—the person who loves to *listen* to music chooses the one who loves to *play* music. Or, they pick someone who shares their interests—two kids who made it to the State Cup in their respective sports decide to team up for lunch. If you had to, Jamie, I bet that you, too, would pick someone who was different or similar to you in some way. As long as we are human, we join together based on these forces of diversity and unity in our own life experience or we relate to these forces in the lives of those we have studied or observed."

Jamie grimaced. All she could think about were her own parents. Two people who couldn't be more opposite—they had even fought about what brand of toothpaste to buy.

Mrs. Flaherty seemed to ignore the look of painful association on Jamie's face. "Similarly," she explained, "The prompt to write an essay about an influential teacher is an experience that people from all over the world have shared for thousands upon thousands of years. For example, we consider Aristotle an influential teacher. And many of the prophets before him."

Jamie decided that if given this assignment, she wouldn't need to go that far back in history. She would write her essay about Mrs. Flaherty.

"Each statement, then, reflects a pervasive social or scientific theme or idea that countless humans have encountered for centuries. Like good poetry, an effective statement is one that people can interpret and respond to in many ways, depending on their own unique experiences."

"I've got a couple ideas for the College Board, Mrs. Flaherty. How about, 'Show whether you agree or disagree with the following statements: Technology frees us in some ways, and enslaves us in others.' Or, 'While necessity is the mother of invention, invention can also breed necessity.'"

For the next few minutes, Jamie continued to share some of the wittier prompts that she, herself, had created upon reading the examples on the College Board website.

Mrs. Flaherty was impressed. "Wow, Jamie! You're really good at this! I especially like the one, 'Support or refute Robert Fulghum's claim that *all I really need to know I learned in kindergarten.*'"

Jamie shrugged. "I guess I can write the question. But can I write the answer?"

"Of course!" Mrs. Flaherty assured her. "As long as you are able to associate between the idea in the statement and what you have lived, read, studied or observed—you walk into that exam with the answers inside of you. Maybe you've noticed that the SAT essay instructions are relatively similar when it comes to describing the kinds of examples to present in your essay."

Mrs. Flaherty peered over Jamie's shoulder at the handout. "In fact," the teacher observed, "almost every statement is followed by the words in bold print, '*Use an example or examples from your experience, readings, studies or observations*' or '*Use an example or examples from history, literature, the arts, current events, politics, science and technology, personal experience or observations.*'" .

"So," Mrs. Flaherty continued, "to address the essay prompt, you can draw information from your own life experience or the lives and communities of others that you have studied, encountered in your readings, or observed in some way."

Jamie wrote in her notebook:

2. Select your Sources of Experience

"Finally," Mrs. Flaherty appeared to be wrapping up her discussion, "Notice that the instructions frequently include the words, **show whether you agree or disagree; support your argument; support your view; challenge, defend, or qualify what is suggested; explain your choice; show in an essay how...; etc.** Each verb—*show*, *agree*, *disagree*, *support*, *challenge*, *defend*, *qualify* and *explain*—is a call for you to express in writing your point of view about the universal theme, idea or experience that is suggested in the statement."

"And you may have noted that the essay instructions frequently contain the reminder, '**explain the reasons for your choice.**' Whatever example or examples of experience you select in response to the statement, you must clearly and convincingly present the reasons or evidence from this experience to defend your view."

Jamie wrote,

3. Write the Persuasive Essay

"In sum," Mrs. Flaherty waited until Jamie's pen was still, "*Collecting information*—which we talked about last week as a major component of the writing process—starts with your choosing an experience or experiences that provide ample information, evidence and details to support, refute or qualify the point that is suggested in the writing prompt. Keep in mind, Jamie, your essay isn't judged on the basis of right or wrong. No one is going to analyze your thoughts. Rather, the essay will be judged overall on your effectiveness at presenting an argument—how well you can define your stance and support it with evidence."

"You've got to admit, Mrs. Flaherty, this is a pretty lengthy list of sources to keep inside of me for an exam. *History, science, technology, literature, politics, current events* and so on. How am I supposed to be an expert on everything?" she asked.

4. If Possible, Draw from Your Own Experience

"No one expects you to be an expert on everything, Jamie. But it would help to walk into that exam with at least one experience or event fresh in your mind. Perhaps your best bet would be first, to draw an example from your own experience—after all, you alone are the expert on your personal life. Your memory is a storehouse filled with years of data on that subject. You can feel comfortable using 'I' in your essay when you are writing from your experience. If your own experience doesn't seem right for the task, then your second best bet might be to identify with an experience from your studies or observations of others.

"For example, perhaps you have recently taken a test on the experience of a famous historical or literary figure. Or, maybe you just wrote a paper and are deeply familiar with the experience of a particular political group or scientific leader. Whether you use your own experience or the experience of others," concluded Mrs. Flaherty, "the key to success is to choose an example of experience that you know well. Ideally, an experience that, upon reflection, is a breeding ground for the thoughts, feelings, and actions you can tie to just about any universal theme or idea."

"You mean like my parents' divorce? Or my experience qualifying for the long-course swimming Junior Olympics? Or what about the literary analysis we had to write on *The Scarlet Letter*? These are things that I know well."

"Yes," said Mrs. Flaherty. "If these are the kinds of experiences that you know inside out, you can associate them with many universal themes—in particular, the one that is suggested in the SAT writing prompt. Let's say you are asked to respond to the statement, 'Two heads are better than one.' Can you think of evidence from your parents' divorce, the Junior Olympics, or *The Scarlet Letter*, to argue for or against the idea, 'two heads are better than one'?"

"I'm not sure," Jamie hesitated. "Wait. Hold on a second. I never would have survived my parents' divorce without the support of my best friend. She was always there for me, listened to all my frustrations. And with the encouragement of my swimming coach, I found the confidence to make it as far as the Junior Olympics while the rest of my life was in shambles. I don't know about *The Scarlet Letter,* unless you argue that two heads *aren't* better than one, especially when they join together to discriminate against Hester, the main character.

"As long as you can present the details and reasons to support your argument, then you can make any kind of association you want, " Mrs. Flaherty replied.

"Hmmm, " Jamie pondered a bit. "So aside from knowing the types of essay assignments on the exam, would it help to walk in there with a couple of experiences fresh in my mind?"

"It couldn't hurt. But I don't mean that you have to *study* or analyze an experience for it to be fresh in your mind. If you have already given something a lot of your thought and attention, then you might find that your ideas and feelings about it bubble more easily to your mind's surface. Or that the details to support your argument seem to flow from your mind automatically.

"For example, what if you were involved in a debate between two student groups? Let's say one group is for spending the extra money in the school budget on a state-of-the-art digital camcorder for the athletics department, and your group is against it because you think the school has other financial priorities. New books for the library, maybe. What if you had to suddenly justify your group's point of view? Would you want some time to prepare your argument?"

"Of course," Jamie said.

"Chances are, you would be in a better position to argue your viewpoint after you had some time to mull over the pro's and con's in your head, and sort through some facts and details in support of buying new books. Thinking on your feet *after* you've had a chance to consider your reasons for buying the books rather than a camcorder would certainly be easier than arguing your case before you've assembled your evidence for it. When you plan your argument, it would be helpful to go with an experience that you have thought about to some extent—in fact, we'll continue this discussion at our next meeting."

"Okay. So I know what kinds of essay assignments may appear on the exam. That'll save me from experiencing five minutes of panic at the beginning. And I know that I don't have to do any prior research to prepare for the essay. The experiences that I can write about are already inside of me. But even if I have plenty of experiences to write about, I do have another problem, Mrs. Flaherty," Jamie sighed. "Whenever I see those writing prompts, my mind becomes all fuzzy or blank. I have a hard time thinking clearly enough to make any associations in the first place."

Mrs. Flaherty sighed, too. "I don't blame you, Jamie," she said. "Some of those prompts can be pretty intimidating—even *I* might be hard pressed to make an immediate association between the prompt and some experience. But like anything else, where there is a will there is a way!

"Jamie, that sounds like a prompt, doesn't it? The next time we meet, I'm going to give you some pointers on planning your response within the first five minutes of writing your essay. Between now and then, here are a couple of strategies to help you practice making quick associations between experiences you have had or observed and the kinds of universal themes or ideas that might appear in an SAT essay prompt. The more you practice making these associations, the easier this task will become for you." Mrs. Flaherty handed Jamie a couple of worksheets that she plucked from a file on her desk.

Jamie chuckled as she skimmed the worksheets. "Will practicing these strategies really make the difference?" she asked.

"Not entirely, " Mrs. Flaherty sighed. "These strategies will strengthen your skills of making associations in the moment—something you will have to do on the SAT essay. The better you are at tying thought-provoking ideas and universal themes to your or others' experience, the easier it will be for you to begin writing and developing your essay.

"But I think you need to address a couple of other issues if you want to get started quickly. In fact, Jamie, I have a pretty good idea of what it takes to write a high-scoring essay, and I even have a specific plan in mind to help you review and practice each ingredient of effective essay writing, one at a time.

"Ingredients?" Jamie wondered if writing an essay could ever be as easy as following a recipe.

"Yes. There are ten ingredients, to be exact. Each ingredient is an action you can take to enhance not just the process but also the content of your writing. If you put these ingredients —or actions—together, you should end up with an effective essay. Ten is a lot, I know, but you can recall these ingredients by remembering that writing is a recursive process. In other words, thinking leads to writing, while the act of writing can further inspire your thinking. Two simple sentences capture this process: *Think to write. Write to think.* I use each letter of the words *think* and *write* to remind me of one essential ingredient or action of essay writing.

"What does the 'T' stand for?" Jamie was already jumping ahead.

Mrs. Flaherty handed Jamie a sheet of paper. On it were written the following headings:

Think to Write—Write to Think

THINK TO WRITE

TRANSFORM YOUR MOOD.

HOP INTO GEAR/S.

IDEATE [Or *Idea*s—Gener*ate* some!]

NARRATE WITH INSIGHT.

KEEP YOUR FOCUS.

WRITE TO THINK

WRITE YOUR INTRO, BODY AND CONCLUSION.

REFLECT ON YOUR EXPERIENCE: TELL.

ILLUSTRATE YOUR EXPERIENCE: SHOW.

TIE TOGETHER WITH TRANSITIONS.

EXPRESS YOUR IDEAS CLEARLY.

"Each day we meet, Jamie, we will discuss one of these letters and the action that it stands for. For starters, I urge you to schedule an appointment with the athletic trainer, Mr. Johnson. He is the best one to talk to you about what the *T* in *Think* stands for: transforming your mood in a way that will help you take control of the writing task. It just so happens that being a trainer is Mr. Johnson's day job. He spends the rest of his time getting his graduate degree in psychology and writing a book on something called 'mental skills coaching.' He can offer you the tips that he gives to his athletes on how to focus more clearly, strengthen their confidence, and push the limits of their performance. He tells me that he himself uses these techniques when he writes his book."

Jamie got up to leave. She had heard good things about Mr. Johnson from her friends who played sports. She would stop by the training room on her way out—he usually hung out there after school when the extracurricular sports activities were in full swing.

"After you've met with Mr. Johnson—come back to me," Mrs. Flaherty called after Jamie. "I've got a few ideas up my sleeve to help you hop into gear and get started with the actual writing of that essay."

"Thanks, Mrs. Flaherty!" Jamie nodded to her teacher.

That evening, Jamie read and practiced the strategies Mrs. Flaherty suggested would help sharpen the skills of association.

Sharpen your Skills of Association

A. Visit a website that provides famous quotations or proverbs, e.g., http://www.famous-quotations.com/; http://www.quotationspage.com/; or http://cogweb.ucla.edu/Discourse/Proverbs/. Each day of the week, do the following:
   1. Choose at least one quotation and/or proverb that you like.
   2. Put the quotation/proverb into your own words.
   3. Then, make at least three associations between what is suggested in the quotation/proverb and what you have experienced, read, studied, or observed.

Jamie's Example:
   1) I like the proverb, *Opposites attract*.
   2) If I put it in my own words, I would say that people who are completely different from each other end up being drawn to one another.
   3) The first association I could make—or the first idea that pops into my head is from my own experience: my best friend and I are as opposite as two people can possibly be, yet our differences make our relationship stronger. Another quick association is to the principal and assistant principal of our school—one is a nit-picky, detail-oriented person while the other is good at skipping the details but seeing the big picture. Together, they make a great team. Finally, I picture my twin cousins. They're fraternal twins and bear no physical resemblance to each other. One is a superstar athlete, and the other is an artist and musician. Yet they are inseparable.

B. Read a feature story from each section of your newspaper. Try to capture the essence of the story with the words of a famous quotation or lesson you have observed from your own or others' experience. Write your own headline for the story that incorporates the words of your quotation or lesson.

Jamie's Examples:
   "Local Girl Scout Troop Learns that Charity Begins at Home"
   "Former Thief Teaches that Honesty is the Best Policy"

C. Choose four or five objects that you can see in your immediate surroundings, or choose objects from the following list:
   1. A glass of water on the table
   2. A book on the shelf
   3. A cluttered desk in the corner
   4. An old answering machine on the counter
   5. A broken clock on the wall

For each object, come up with questions that reveal contrasting views of the object, and force you to draw some meaning from that object—no matter how silly. Don't hesitate to use famous quotations, puns, proverbs, etc., in your questions.

Jamie's Examples:
- A glass of water on the table: "Is it better to describe the glass as half empty or half full?"
- A book on the shelf: "Can I judge this book by its cover? Or do I need to look at what's inside?"
- A cluttered desk in the corner: "Does a cluttered desk mean a cluttered mind? Or a creative mind?"
- An answering machine on the counter: "Is life more stressful with an answering machine or without it?"
- A broken clock on the wall: "If I were a broken clock, would I think that time stands still for me or that it keeps going?"

Part 2

T.H.I.N.K. To Write

Chapter Four

Transform your Mood—Part 1

Mrs. Flaherty knew that composing an essay when the time is limited and the stakes are high could cause even the best of writers to recoil in panic. She also knew that managing such anxiety is similar to what athletes, dramatic artists, and rescue workers do to perform under stress. Whether writing the SAT essay, running a race, acting on stage, or handling a crisis—people who deal with their anxiety in constructive ways are likely to perform more effectively than those who allow their anxiety to erode their confidence and concentration.

Anxiety—How Can You Put It to Use?

Consider, for example, Kalin's and Jamie's approaches to the SAT essay task. One of the key differences between them was the way in which each managed her anxiety. While Kalin was swimming in self-doubt, Jamie felt positive about the challenge facing her. Mrs. Flaherty had known that after a few sessions with Mr. Johnson, the "mental skills" coach, Jamie would learn to tolerate and control her anxiety, then channel it as energy toward taking the exam.

On the other hand, Kalin's anxiety clouded her thinking. Rather than use it to her benefit, Kalin allowed her anxiety to become a negative force. She was spending precious seconds breaking pencils and spitting out eraser grit—behaviors out of frustration that drained her energy and distracted her from the task at hand.

Of course, Jamie, too, had her moments of doubt. The idea that her essay was being timed and judged made her uncomfortable. But after her previous negative experience writing the SAT essay, Jamie resolved that she would find a way to prevent her anxiety from consuming her thoughts. She remembered that last time, the voice inside her head was shouting over and over, "Hurry up! You can't waste time!" And when she read the essay prompt, her fear only intensified. "Great. You can't even think. You can't even understand the question. You are never going to finish in time!" Jamie had been unable to snap out of her growing state of doom, panic, and self-deprecation.

Managing Your Anxiety

In her first visit to Mr. Johnson, Jamie attempted to explain her predicament: "I know I shouldn't be as intimidated by the exam the next time I face it, because now I have a pretty good grasp of the types of questions that will be asked, and what is expected of me in response. But I still feel a pit inside my stomach. What if ..."

"You've already taken the first step, Jamie," Mr. Johnson broke in. "The more you know what to expect, the less fear you will feel. That's why sports teams watch tapes of their opponents' games, or practice at the game site beforehand so they can have a sense of what to expect. Any action you take to learn about the situation before you face it will give you a greater sense of control."

"But I'm still terrified that being familiar with the writing task isn't enough. I want to be able to tackle the essay without wasting time—to jump right into it. I know I can write. I'm afraid, though, that the second I see the test, those little doubts will become bigger and bigger and take over. Knowing what is expected of me on the exam won't do me much good if I'm in a state of panic. I remember what happened last time. I wanted to throw up. My head pounded. My brain froze. The last thing I could do was write." From somewhere inside her stomach, Jamie could feel the familiar pangs of doubt.

Mr. Johnson chuckled. "I know what you mean. I remember feeling that way many times in high school and college. Every once in awhile I still have these crazy dreams—even nightmares—about taking exams. For example, I discover that the questions on the test are written in a language I've never heard of. Or I dream that I oversleep and wake up after the exam has started. Or something happens to prevent me from getting to the test on time. Or maybe I show up to the exam room on time, but no one is there. Then I run around the entire building, frantically trying to find where the test is located." Shaking his head, Mr. Johnson admitted, "Even as an adult, exams still bring out some of my worst fears and anxieties."

"You mean you *still* take exams?" Jamie was incredulous. The thought of having to take exams until she was old was a frightening one.

"You bet. Even in grad school, I have to take exams. And beyond grad school—to get a license in my profession—I'll have to take more tests. Many of them involve papers and essays. But I'll tell you, Jamie, what helps me now—something that took me years to figure out—is the simple realization that my anxiety is absolutely normal. I believe that a large part of it is actually a sign of my growth as a writer. And you may be experiencing similar growing pains.

"You see, the more we develop our writing skills, the more writing means to us. It becomes an expression of our inner selves. If we want to become better writers, we have to let go, take risks, find ways to organize the complexity of our ideas, practice different techniques, strengthen our style, find the right words to expose our thoughts and feelings to others and...," Mr. Johnson took a breath, "...ultimately, be judged by what we write. No wonder we feel anxious. It's natural to."

"Wait, Mr. Johnson." Jamie interrupted. "I want to remember what you are saying, and I feel like I'm going to miss something if I don't write it down. I know this isn't a class, but do you mind if I take notes?" Without waiting for a response, she opened her backpack with a loud *zip*, and pulled out a pad and pen.

Mr. Johnson paused for a moment, as if he was on stage waiting for the applause to die down. Jamie grabbed a chair next to him, plopped down with the pad on her lap, and poised her pen to write. "Okay," she nodded.

Mr. Johnson continued. "Besides the growing importance of writing to me, I can think of several reasons why I have been anxious during essay exams over the years. For one, time constraints rattle me. Sometimes I can almost hear the clock ticking away inside my head. Plus, knowing that I'll be graded inhibits my thinking.

"Also, I don't always feel confident about my writing skills. For example, maybe I have to write a persuasive essay and I am not used to that particular kind of writing. Then, my anxiety is likely to skyrocket. Even my own self-talk, or what I say to myself when I am trying to write, can get in the way. I might convince myself that I don't know what the teacher wants, and end up so frustrated that I lose all sense of purpose.

"Or sometimes I just don't care all that much about what I am assigned to write. I guess I'm the type who has a hard time getting excited about comparing the images of light and darkness in seven texts by medieval writers. I cannot count all the literary analyses I had to do on books or poems that failed to speak to me. I am much more motivated to write when I can get into the topic—when it has some meaning to me, or when I, myself, can choose it."

Jamie's hand started to ache from taking notes. She shook her fingers. But Mr. Johnson spoke with such passion; the ache didn't really bother her. She mustered all the energy she could to capture his next words.

"It took me some time and a lot of trial and error to get a sense of my own writing process. Turns out I was doing some things that blocked, rather than fueled my writing. Like trying too hard to stick to rules and formulas, when what I really needed to do was loosen up, trust myself, and trust the process."

"Trust the process? I don't get it...."

"Well, I was trying too hard. When all I had to do was let go. Once I let go, the words came. They came from a place deep inside of me and maybe beyond me. Like a big silver trout up out of deep water."

Jamie knew exactly what Mr. Johnson meant. She loved to fish at her Uncle's cabin on the shores of Sturgeon Lake in upstate Minnesota. Whenever she caught a big one, it always seemed to tug just at the moment she was about to reel in her line for the day. The moment she was about to give up. The fish came when she was least expecting it. Out of the water's depths. Like a surprise visitor from a world beneath the foamy waves gently sloshing at the surface.

"So if you were so anxious, how did you get to that point where you could let go of all that anxiety and write?" Jamie put down her pen and slid to the edge of her seat. She wondered, "How could Mr. Johnson know so well what she, herself, had such a hard time putting into words?"

"I've learned three things, Jamie. First, by realizing that your anxiety is normal, you know to expect it. Keep in mind, it's not the anxiety, itself, that is debilitating. It's how you *respond* to it. Everyone 'has' anxiety, but some deal with it more effectively than others. If you expect anxiety, you can better prepare for it, and avoid being its victim."

"Second, I've found it helpful to do a little 'reframing' of anxiety. In other words, I try to change my perception of it. I try to cast my anxiety in a positive light. We tend to think of anxiety in unpleasant terms. Those uncomfortable sensations we get before something possibly bad is about to happen. What do *you* feel, Jamie, in response to the word *anxiety*? What pops into your head?"

"Hmmm," Jamie shrugged. "Fear or worry, I guess."

"Yep. For many of us, anxiety means fear, worry, dread, tension, or even loss of control. After all, in moments of excessive anxiety, the body may fail to do what the mind tells it. Or the mind stops thinking clearly. As a result, a person 'chokes.' Our performance suffers.

"However, just as anxiety occurs in anticipation of something 'bad,' and the anxiety, itself, gets in the way of what we are doing—anxiety can also lead to something good. Franklin Roosevelt put it nicely in his First Inaugural address back in 1933. 'The only thing we have to fear is fear itself.' He said this during the Great Depression—a time when fear and uncertainty swept the nation. People were out of work and the banks closed. Some weren't sure of their next meal. Yet, with the help of Roosevelt's New Deal, we created a lot of work opportunities to spur our nation's growth. Some of our greatest expansion efforts took place between 1933 and 1937.

"The point is, our country took positive action in the face of anxiety. Just because we feel anxiety, Jamie, that doesn't mean the outcome has to be negative. Like FDR, I believe in the power of perception. I like to perceive anxiety in a more constructive than destructive light. I like to reframe it as a sign of future possibility. A sign that something positive can happen. I like to think that anxiety can fuel our greatest performance."

Jamie's pen remained still as she tried to digest Mr. Johnson's words and relate them to the SAT essay.

"For example," he explained, as if sensing Jamie's need to tie all this to the SAT, "if I feel anxious, I have a number of choices. Instead of controlling my anxiety, I can let it control me. I can allow my frustration to cloud my thinking and block my writing. I can panic, run from the exam room, and maybe avoid the test forever. Or I can learn to tolerate and control my anxiety and create positive results. This is the approach you are already taking toward the SAT, Jamie. Otherwise, we wouldn't be sitting here."

Jamie nodded with a thoughtful look in her eye. Her pen remained still. She knew she had some questions for Mr. Johnson on this point. But he continued to talk with a thoughtful look in *his* eye.

"Another choice," mulled Mr. Johnson, "Is facing the experience and if it is beyond our control, learning to make the most of the negative consequences. I just read that the U.S. women's 2003 World Cup soccer team watched a tape of their last defeat with Sweden before facing them again in the World Cup. They felt all over again what it was like to lose, and were so determined not to repeat that agonizing experience that it made them stronger. Watching a replay of their defeat actually helped them beat Sweden in 2003—kind of like what the philosopher, Nietzsche, had to say: 'Whatever does not destroy me makes me stronger.' You are taking this approach with the SAT, too, Jamie. Thanks to your choking on the last exam, I guarantee you will become a stronger writer."

"Nietzsche's quote would make a great prompt for the SAT essay." Jamie smiled. One day, she could write an essay about this whole experience. But now, she wondered how remembering the agony of her last essay exam might make her stronger. Just recalling her feelings of panic and self-doubt made her anxious all over again.

"Or, as I said," Mr. Johnson went on, his voice rescuing Jamie from her growing gloom, "I can avoid the experience that causes me anxiety. I can ignore it, skip it altogether by refusing to sign up for the test in the first place. I can postpone it until later, or ask someone else who doesn't feel as much anxiety to take my place in the experience. Of course, this option might work okay if I were asking someone to sub for me on the baseball field. I don't think it would go over big if you got a sub to take your SAT."

Jamie smiled again and with renewed fervor, tried to record each of Mr. Johnson's ideas on her notepad.

"Third, I've learned the hard way that if anxiety gets in the way of what you want to do, you've got to ask yourself, 'What is out of balance?' Overanxiety may mean you care too much, whereas underanxiety, or outright indifference, may mean you care too little. After all, Jamie, you wouldn't be here today if you hadn't—as you explained—'panicked' during the last exam. You obviously care a lot about something. That experience of panic had a message in it."

"I guess you are right," Jamie sighed. "When you say 'out of balance,' I know what you mean. I think I must be making the SAT essay out to be bigger than it really is. Sometimes I feel like my whole college career—my future—depends on it. Everyone talks about the SAT score as being a deciding factor in admissions. But is that really true? I think it is only a tiny piece of who I am. I don't want to go to a school that sees me mainly as a score on an exam."

"So putting the essay in perspective is important." Mr. Johnson agreed. "In the whole geopolitical scheme of things," he laughed, "your essay is not a life-and-death concern. And keep in mind, the raters that grade your essay are probably the first to admit that they don't expect perfection in twenty-five minutes. Rather, they expect to see a rough, unpolished first draft. They expect to see mistakes. If *they* realize that thou art a mere mortal and your essay isn't up for the Pulitzer Prize, so can you!"

"There's something else," Jamie admitted. She took a deep breath. "Like you, I need to work on writing a persuasive essay. I've only done it a couple of times, and never under time constraints. Although I always thought I was a decent writer, maybe in this situation, my skills aren't up to the challenge."

"So let's try a couple of things." Mr. Johnson suggested. "First, we'll practice what it's like to expect anxiety; but from now on, we'll 'reframe' it as a form of energy or intensity that can fuel your performance and lead to a positive outcome. The goal is to figure out the amount of anxiety that works for you—just the 'right' level of anxiety that actually contributes to your performance. Then you can be ready for your anxiety and when you feel it, you can adjust it to your advantage. Like turning the thermostat up or down to adjust the temperature.

"Second, we need to work on making the task of writing an essay in twenty-five minutes less overwhelming. We can start by breaking it down into small, manageable pieces. That is something that both Mrs. Flaherty and I figured we could help you with.

"How about spending our next session—or however long it takes—exploring ways to use the intensity you feel before the exam or any other stressful event, for that matter, to your advantage? In other words, just like the athlete, you can discover what it takes to perform 'in the zone.'"

"Sounds great!" Jamie exclaimed, but beneath the enthusiasm was a pit of uncertainty about what lay in store for her.

"I know I've been talking quite a bit. But before you go, let's just summarize some of the key points we've raised, Jamie."

"I've written them down—or most of them, I hope!" Jamie offered. "I may have changed your wording a little, but this is what I got out of our talk." She read from her list:

> ### Mr. Johnson's Mental Skills Pointers:
> - The more you know what to expect, the less anxiety you will feel. *Any* action you take to learn about the situation before you face it will give you a greater sense of control.
> - Anxiety is normal. It is actually a sign of our growth as writers, showing the increasing importance we attach to our writing, and the risks we take as writers.
>
> **Things that get in the way of our writing:**
> - Time constraints.
> - Knowing that we will be graded on what we write.
> - Knowing, deep inside, that we need more practice in a particular area of writing (like persuasive essays.)
> - Our own self-talk, especially the negative self-talk.
> - Having little care or interest about the topic.
> - Sticking too hard to rules and formulas, then feeling scared when they don't help me.
>
> **Three lessons about anxiety:**
> - <u>Anxiety is normal</u>. Expect it so I can prepare for it and avoid being its victim.
> - <u>Reframe anxiety,</u> or change its meaning. Think of anxiety in a positive vs. negative light. Just as anxiety might get in the way of what I am doing and lead to a negative experience, it might also result in a good experience and fuel my greatest performance.
> - To help ease my anxiety, <u>put the essay in proper perspective</u>. It is not a life-or-death concern. It is not the deciding factor in my future, although it may seem that way. I am more than an SAT score. And worst-case scenario, if I do poorly, it is not the end of the world. I have chances to take the exam again, and time to practice my writing. Besides, according to Nietzsche, I'll end up a stronger person.

"Wow!" Mr. Johnson was impressed. "Your notes are a lot more concise than my talking. I would love a copy of them so I can remember my own advice!"

"Sure, Mr. Johnson. Thanks again. I'll be back next week, same time."

Jamie gathered her belongings and started to weave her way through the haphazard rows of chairs and exercise equipment.

"You know, Jamie," Mr. Johnson mused as Jamie reached the door. "This talk is good for me, too. It's like talking to myself aloud! I need to remember this stuff to get me through grad school. It applies to so many things—much more than to just an essay exam. So I need to thank you, too."

Jamie was relieved that Mr. Johnson also seemed to be getting something out of their session. "See you next week!" she smiled. She would be ready. Ready to use her anxiety to help rather than hinder her writing process, and maybe to lure that silver trout from the water's depths.

Chapter Five

Hop into Gear/s

After meeting with Mr. Johnson, draping the school gym with streamers for Friday's Homecoming Dance, attempting to eat her Dad's overly nuked chicken-pot pie, and doing her homework (well, most of it), Jamie snuggled into bed with her laptop. The time had come for her to do what she did best: electronic multitasking.

Within seconds, Jamie was in her element. Her fingers flew as she checked her email and IM'd her friends. She looked at who had commented on her FaceBook page and she watched a video clip of Susan Boyle's latest hit on YouTube. In between the chimes of IM's, she also surfed the College Board website for new sample SAT essay assignments.

At **www.collegeboard.com,** Jamie read some student essays prompted by the question, "Do memories hinder or help people in their effort to learn from the past and succeed in the present?" At first, she couldn't believe that average students were capable of answering such a deep question under time pressure. But the College Board posted a bunch of responses written by actual students. Jamie found an essay for each possible score ranging from 1, the lowest, to 6, the highest. Jamie figured if she had to respond to this prompt, her essay could definitely represent one of the lower scores.

Over the next week, Jamie read some more sample prompts and student essays in the SAT preparation book section of her school library.

After reading a bunch of SAT writing prompts, Jamie found herself making them up out of nowhere. Prompts popped into her head while she was serving the volleyball in gym class, taking a shower, or even waiting in line at the school cafeteria to buy a strawberry smoothie.

Before long her mind was churning out prompts every bit as compelling as the ones on the real SAT's. Some were humorous, others serious. Jamie knew that making them up was a first step toward dealing with her SAT anxiety—becoming familiar with the concepts so that she would know what to expect. This sense of what to expect could save precious time in the exam situation. It could save her from having to freak out for several minutes.

Writing in Flow

"So, Jamie, how did the session go with Mr. Johnson?" Mrs. Flaherty asked at their next meeting.

"Pretty well, " Jamie smiled. "You were right. We didn't do any actual writing. I guess that's not what you sent me to Mr. Johnson for, anyway. He's helping me figure out how to manage my anxiety."

"Good," Mrs. Flaherty said, "it's what we mean by the *t* in *think*—'transforming your mood.'"

"Right," Jamie said. "I know a lot about moods!"

"What did he say you should do?" Mrs. Flaherty aked.

"Well, he told me to think of anxiety as a positive force rather than allow it to become a distraction. You know, I never really considered my nervousness to be a good thing. Usually, it grows worse and worse and then I kind of panic. Mr. Johnson says my nervousness is a form of *intensity* and a sign that I care about what I write.

"To be honest," Jamie admitted, "I don't understand exactly what Mr. Johnson is going to do next. He says he'll show me how to adjust my anxiety like a thermostat so I can use it to my advantage. If he can do that," Jamie said, shaking her head, "he'll help me with a lot more than just writing!"

Jamie's thoughts instantly jumped to her parents and all the nasty bickering after their divorce. To feel instant anxiety, all she needed to do was think about her home life, her *two* home lives. She pictured her life at her Dad's dingy apartment, and then she saw their house—well now it was her Mom's house—with a *For Sale* sign on the front lawn. She felt her heart speeding up and couldn't stop it.

"Hmmm," Mrs. Flaherty nodded. "Controlling anxiety is a skill you can apply to many situations. I'd love to see how he teaches that. Did Mr. Johnson mention that one way to handle anxiety is to break down a task, such as writing, into small, manageable parts?"

"Yeah. Mr. Johnson said that both of you would help me to break down … break it down… I mean…." Jamie lost her train of thought.

"Break down the *task*, Jamie—not you—into small, manageable parts." Mrs. Flaherty smiled. "We want to help you enter what is called the *flow* state."

"Enter the what?" Jamie asked, her mind on other things.

"The *flow* state. A term used by the psychologist, Mihaly Csik… Csikszent…—I always have a hard time remembering his name—so I better break *it* down into smaller parts. Csik—szent—mi—hal—yi. That's it. Dr. Csikszentmihalyi, in his book, *Flow: The Psychology of Optimal Experience*. He says that when people fully engage in an activity, they sometimes enter what is called *flow*. You might be in flow when you're playing the flute, or totally absorbed in a chess game, or determined to beat your best time in the one-hundred-yard butterfly.

Whatever the activity, your heart and will are so into it that your mind has no room for distraction. You know clearly what your goals are in the situation, though you're not really 'thinking' them. And you can feel how well you are doing. Writing an essay is a perfect example of a possible *flow* experience. You can become so deeply involved in the process that you forget the clock and the world around you. All that matters is making your inner voice come to life on paper."

"Really?" Jamie asked, not sure she believed writing a timed essay could bring on flow. "Mr. Johnson mentioned athletes' performing 'in the zone,'" she said. "Is being 'in the zone' the same as 'flow'?"

"Yes! And you don't have to be an athlete to experience what it is like 'in the zone.' If I am in the zone while teaching, I have to ask a student to inform me when the bell goes off at the end of class. I don't even hear it. Just like the state of flow, I can be in the zone while working. Time disappears. I look at the clock and realize with a start that my poor kids are still waiting for me to pick them up and chauffeur them to soccer practice.

"If I enter the zone while writing at nighttime, the next thing I know the birds are singing and sunlight is streaming through my window. Once I get into my writing, I find it difficult to stop. Instinct drives my words. I don't actually think that much; in fact, I forget myself and allow the ideas to flow.

"The more I let go, the more my thoughts and feelings merge, and the more the words bubble out of me effortlessly. I remember the world champion skater, Michelle Kwan, once said on TV that when she skates her best, when she skates with the most passion, she feeds off the excitement of her audience. I, too, sense my connection with an audience when I express myself. And I know that the energy of that bond fuels my best work."

"I've felt that way, too," Jamie said. "It happens to me when I get really involved in a school project—like when I'm writing a term paper or a poem for the school magazine."

"So you see, Jamie, you can enter 'the zone' or a state of 'flow' when you write," Mrs. Flaherty said. There was a social psychologist named Susan Perry who was so fascinated with this idea that she wrote a book called *Writing in Flow*. She interviewed professional writers to learn what helped them enter the flow state while writing. A few of them described the importance of 'automating their working habits.' In other words, they engaged in a particular routine that enabled them to ease right into the writing process."

"Like what?" Jamie asked.

"Ernest Hemmingway sharpened pencils in his Paris flat," Mrs. Flaherty said. Some writers might play music before sitting down to write, or focus on writing the next sentence only and not the entire end product. These patterns of thinking and behavior are what help some writers get started. Imagine that writing a timed essay is like being in a race, and you jump off the starting block the moment the task is revealed. Within seconds, your mind and body shift into gear and become absorbed in the activity of writing—like swimming or riding a bike. You do them automatically, without thinking. All you need is to start kicking or pedaling your feet in a particular direction for your mind and body to take control. After a few minutes, you are in flow."

Mrs. Flaherty paused for a moment, as if to remember where she was headed with her explanation. "So how does entering flow relate to the SAT essay?" Mrs. Flaherty looked at Jamie, her eyes inviting her to draw a connection.

"Well," Jamie replied, "I guess I could come up with my own routine to start writing. I could figure out a couple of steps to automatically ease myself into it."

"Right," Mrs. Flaherty nodded. "Like the writers in Susan Perry's book, you can try different ways to get started—ways that, with repeated practice, you can rely on to occur automatically because they have become second nature to you. And by engaging yourself in the simplest, smallest steps of writing—one at a time—the less energy and attention you have to devote to outside distractions, nagging thoughts, or anxieties about being graded."

"Sort of like the Nike slogan—'*Just do it*'? But what is *it* that I *just do*?" Jamie asked. "I know that I need to *start* writing as soon as possible. After all, I only have twenty-five minutes!"

The Mechanics of Getting Started

"For the start of your writing process to be automatic, I can suggest some useful steps that work for many writers. First, let me ask you a question. What do drivers of standard-shift cars use when they start their ignitions?"

"What?" Jamie asked. She knew very little about standard-shift cars. Didn't her grandfather drive one long ago? The car with the big stick jutting from the floor between the front seats? Jamie remembered those cracked red leather seats. They had scratched her skin and smelled of ancient sweat.

"Gears. They shift their gears." Mrs. Flaherty said. "Remember I showed you that the *h* in *think* stands for *hop into GEAR/S*? Just as we use the word *think* to remind us of the process of our writing, each letter of the word G-E-A-R-S reminds me of a step to take or key question to answer to get started on my essay or automatically shift into my writing process. Rather than think in terms of my entire response to the essay prompt—that's way too overwhelming—I break my essay down into smaller, more manageable responses to five simple, key questions."

Jamie watched as Mrs. Flaherty walked over to the blackboard and grabbed a fat piece of purple chalk from the tray. She wrote GEARS in large letters, setting up a formula of sorts:

G = **G**oal
E = **E**xample/s of experience
A = **A**rgument
R = **R**easons
S = **S**upporting Evidence and Details

After reading the list, Jamie still looked puzzled.

"Do you have an SAT essay prompt that we can use right now?" Mrs. Flaherty asked. "That would help me explain how GEARS can help your writing get off to an automatic start, without getting distracted by anxiety."

Jamie fumbled in her backpack, pulling out a file thick with papers. "Here's a sample question," she said, handing Mrs. Flaherty her most recent printout on SAT essays that she had retrieved from the Internet.

"Great. Now I am going to do something unusual. I'm going to invite you inside my head. I am going to think out loud so you'll know what I must say to myself to hop into gears. In other words, you'll hear my self-talk—the voice that coaches me through the start of my writing process."

Inside Mrs. Flaherty's Brain

Mrs. Flaherty read aloud for Jamie the prompt at the top of the page:
"One step forward, two steps backward.

The phrase above suggests that a positive development in one area may cause a setback in another area. Or, progress is harder to make than it first appears. Or, in the words of Clare Boothe Luce, 20th century U.S. playwright and politician: No good deed goes unpunished. In an essay, show whether you agree or disagree with the above statement. To support your argument, use an example or examples from history, science and technology, politics, literature, the arts, current events, or your personal experience."

"Okay," Jamie's teacher continued. "Before I even allow myself time to get anxious, I immediately think of the first letter **G** in **GEARS**. It reminds me of the key word, ***goal***, in a fundamental question,

'What is the* goal *of this writing task? What am I asked to do here?'

"Hmmm," Mrs. Flaherty continued aloud. "I realize that the goal of this assignment is to either agree, disagree, or both agree AND disagree with the phrase *'One step forward, two steps backward.'* If I agree, the goal of my essay would be to show that a step forward is often followed by two steps backwards. To me, this statement means that progress is hard earned. On the other hand, if I disagree—the goal of my essay would be to show that a step forward is NOT necessarily followed by two steps backwards. That is, a positive development is not such a challenge.

While trying to keep up with Mrs. Flaherty's stream of consciousness, Jamie couldn't help but notice that her rambling, intellectual tone had a familiar ring to it, and that her hair was as red and curly as ... "That's it! After two years, I finally realize who Mrs. Flaherty reminds me of!" she thought. "Ms. Frizzle from *The Magic School Bus books*. A Language Arts version of Ms. Frizzle!" Jamie imagined that Mrs. Flaherty was a mere two inches tall, and covered from head to toe with purple chalk dust.

Mrs. Flaherty must have observed the distant, slightly amused expression in Jamie's eyes. "So!" she cut herself short. "Just to get myself started, I'll write on my paper..."

Jamie tried to refocus her attention on the chalkboard. But her imagination was in overdrive. She visualized a miniature version of herself peering out the window of a matchbox-sized vehicle. Was it the magic schoolbus? No, it was her grandfather's old stick shift! In her mind's eye, Jamie was driving along a strange, neon-lit skyway that looked like the picture of neural pathways in her textbook on the brain.

Mrs. Flaherty wrote on the board:

Goal = To show that _____

"Whether I am ready to fill in the blank or not doesn't matter at this point. All that matters is that I have just set my first important goal. I have told my brain that I must prove, disprove, or qualify the statement in the essay prompt."

"Next," she continued, "I turn to the *E* in **GEARS,** which reminds me of a key word in the *second* question I need to answer,

'What EXAMPLE/S of EXPERIENCE (from my own life, observation, or reading) can I use in my essay?'

Jamie heard Mrs. Flaherty's voice as if it were echoing inside a cavern:

"For now, all I have to do is tell my brain that I need to come up with a good example or examples of experience so I can develop a strong argument in my essay. For the sake of simplicity, I'm going to try to come up with one experience—one experience that I know quite well. Remember what we talked about at our last meeting, Jamie? Come up with a memory of an experience you can describe in detail? If I have mulled over that experience for some time, and it is fresh in my mind—then I can more easily think about it on my feet the day of the exam and pull from it ample evidence and details to support or refute the idea, *"One step forward, two steps backward."*

Mrs. Flaherty wrote on the board,

Example/s of Experience = _____.

"By drawing the line after *experience*, my brain gets the message to start digging for examples that fit the prompt."

Mrs. Flaherty pointed to the **A** in GEARS. "Now this letter prompts me to think about another crucial question: 'What's my ARGUMENT?'

"If the goal of my essay is to prove or disprove the statement, *'A step forward can be followed by two steps backwards,'* I must take a position and give my line of reasoning for it. This is my essay's **argument**. Keep in mind, merely stating my opinion about the statement is not enough.

"In my essay, I must back up my argument with evidence. A convincing essay, then, is one in which I present the evidence and details to support the main ideas of my argument. In essay writing, we sometimes call this specific argument a "thesis statement." For now, all I want to remind my brain is that my essay needs an argument—my point of view and the main reasons behind my thinking. So I go back to my goal, decide on the position I want to take based on my example/s of experience, and write,

Argument = my position _____ + the line of reasoning for my position."

"I am all set now," Mrs. Flaherty smiled, "To move on to the **R** in

GEARS. As you may already have guessed, **R** suggests a key word in the question, *'What are the REASONS in my argument?'*

Each reason answers the question, 'Why?' For example, what are my **reasons—the line of reasoning**—for arguing that two steps backwards follow a step forward? Usually a good rule of thumb is to come up with at least three reasons for my specific argument, position, opinion, or point of view—in other words, three answers to the question, 'Why?' To serve as a reminder, I write on my paper,

    Reasons =   1) _____
                        2) _____
                        3) _____

Finally, I want to send a message to my brain for a few more pieces of information. I need *supporting evidence and details* to back up the reasons for my position. A good example of experience should be rich with specific evidence and details. Think of lawyers who must argue their cases in court. The clearer their evidence, the stronger their cases. Evidence is what enables them to convince the jury to believe their point of view. For example, if I were prosecuting a man who was accused of murder, my case would certainly be strong if I had a murder weapon with his fingerprints on it, several witnesses who observed him commit the murder in broad daylight, and proof that he had a motive to kill—perhaps the victim had served time in jail for viciously attacking the defendant's wife."

Jamie's eyes widened.

"So the final **S** in **GEARS** reminds me of a key word in my fifth and final question,

'To develop my argument, what <u>SUPPORTING EVIDENCE</u> or <u>DETAILS</u> can I present?'

On my paper, I go back to the three reasons in my argument, and attach lines for the evidence or supporting details that contribute to each reason. Like this:

Reason #1 = _____   _____ **Supporting Evidence and Details:**

_____ **Supporting Evidence and Details:**

Reason #2 = _____   _____

_____ **Supporting Evidence and Details:**

Reason #3 = _____   _____

So you see, Jamie, my **supporting evidence and details** lead directly to the **reasons** I use to convince my reader of my point of view. After answering these five questions, my final self-talk should boil down to at least one example of experience and at least three reasons and the supporting evidence to support the argument I will develop in my essay. With practice, the answers to my five questions become an automatic script I say to myself in my head:

> *The **goal** of this assignment is to present an argument in agreement or disagreement or both with the phrase, 'one step forward, two steps backwards.' Drawing from my **example/s of experience**,_____, I will **argue** my position that _____ because_____ _____, and _____ (three reasons from my experience). The **evidence and details** I will use to **support** each **reason** in my **argument** are _____, _____, _____, _____, _____, etc.*

Now that I have laid out the information I need to structure my response to the essay assignment, I can start brainstorming about what I will write." Mrs. Flaherty looked at Jamie, who sat silently.

Jamie was completely wiped out by Mrs. Flaherty's example.. It was like a stream of consciousness exercise but with all sorts of rules. Wanting to be polite, she kept her thoughts to herself: *Mrs. Flaherty is giving me an awful lot of information to digest at once. Too much. At least the word GEARS helps to break it all down. But what does the **G** stand for again?*

Mrs. Flaherty gave Jamie a reassuring smile, as if to read her thoughts. "This is going to take a little practice, Jamie. But trust me. I'll give you the GEARS guidelines. Read through them until you can remember, without looking, what each letter represents. Together, they provide the direction for what you will write. A way to map out your essay. In essence, GEARS helps you plan the argument that will drive your essay forward. Remember the Hayes and Flower model that we talked about a few days ago? Planning is a vital step of the writing process, and hopping into GEARS gets you started."

Pulling from the pile of papers on her desk, Mrs. Flaherty handed Jamie some worksheets. "The next time you come," she challenged, "I'll ask you to tell me from memory what G, E, A, R, and S prompt you to think about while planning your essay."

Jamie took a moment to look at the first page. "Okay." She accepted Mrs. Flaherty's challenge. "If I can remember ROY G. BIV, the boy's name I learned in kindergarten to help me remember red, orange, yellow, green, blue, indigo, violet—the colors of the spectrum—GEARS shouldn't be too difficult."

"Believe it or not, Jamie, I still remember the native American name, SOH CAH TOA, after over four decades. My ninth grade geometry teacher, Mrs. Ruthen, taught it to us to remember the formulas for the sins, cosins, and tangents of a triangle."

Jamie smiled. *Four decades was forever!* She looked at the second worksheet and observed the same collection of blanks that Mrs. Flaherty had scrawled in purple chalk across the board. Glancing at the clock, she saw that it was just about time to catch the after-school bus. "So the bottom line is, rather than allowing myself to be overwhelmed by the essay assignment, I should immediately break the task down into small steps by telling my brain to think about GEARS."

"That's it." Mrs. Flaherty recited one more time, "Goal, example/s of experience, argument, reasons and supporting evidence."

"Then," Jamie continued, "Once I've laid out my GEARS roadmap, I can go back and fill in the blanks, or respond to each question," she pointed to the worksheet. "Right?"

"Right," Mrs. Flaherty said. *This is going to call for some brainstorming. Something I'll teach more about in our next session.*

"Okay," Jamie said. "I'll at least have a plan for my essay ready to fill in."

"And when you get good at this, you'll be able to figure out the guidelines for your entire essay in less than two minutes."

"I've heard of outlines for essays, not guidelines," Jamie said.

"By guidelines, I mean something a little more flexible," Mrs. Flaherty explained. "I like to think of guidelines as signposts along the way, but not the way, itself. When you have only twenty-five minutes to write your essay, you need to get off to a quick start and at the same time, start with some sense of direction. A few small steps of planning help you do both. The next time we meet, we'll talk more about brainstorming and coming up with the ideas to fill in these blanks."

"Thanks," Jamie smiled. She loaded her gear into her already bulging backpack and was off. Like the kid in Ms. Frizzle's Magic School Bus, she too had a school bus to catch.

HOP INTO *GEARS*

G = **G**oal
E = **E**xample/s of experience
A = **A**rgument
R = **R**easons
S = **S**upporting Evidence and Details

1. GOAL
What is the *goal* of this writing task? What am I asked to do here?

2. EXAMPLE/S OF EXPERIENCE
What EXAMPLE/S of EXPERIENCE (from my own life, observations or reading) can I use in my essay?

3. ARGUMENT
What's my ARGUMENT (my position and/or line of reasoning)?

4. REASONS
What are the specific REASONS for my argument? (Think of three).

5. SUPPORTING EVIDENCE AND DETAILS
To develop my argument, what SUPPORTING EVIDENCE or DETAILS (from my example/s of experience) can I present? (Think of three specific pieces of evidence and/or details to support each reason).

AUTOMATIC SELF-TALK SCRIPT (SAMPLE 1):

The goal of this assignment is to present an argument that agrees and/or disagrees with the statement, _____. Drawing from my example/s of experience_____, I will argue my position/point of view that _____ because (of) _____, _____, and _____ (three reasons from my experience). The evidence and details I will use to support each reason in my argument are _____, _____, _____; _____, _____,_____; and _____,_____, _____.

AUTOMATIC SELF-TALK SCRIPT (SAMPLE 2):

The goal of this assignment is to show in an essay how/why/that _____ _____. Drawing from my example/s of experience_____, I will prove my position/point of view that _____ because _____, _____, and _____ (three reasons from my experience). The evidence and details I will use to support each reason in my argument are _____, _____, _____; _____, _____,_____; and _____,_____, _____.

YOUR OWN SELF-TALK SCRIPT:

The goal of this assignment is to _____

Fill in your own GEARS self-talk.

HOPPING INTO *GEARS*: WHAT'S MY PLAN?

SELF-TALK SCRIPT:

Goal—To show in an essay that _____ [based on my]
Example/s of Experience _____

Argument = My position_____ + the line of
reasoning for my position _____

For my argument:

                                                    Supporting Evidence and Details:

Reason # 1 = _____   _____

                                                    Supporting Evidence and Details:

Reason # 2 = _____   _____

                                                    Supporting Evidence and Details:

Reason # 3 = _____   _____

Chapter Six
Transforming Your Mood-Part II

"Hey, Jamie! Come on in and have a seat!" Mr. Johnson called from the stationary bicycle. The small gym was teeming with students doing their workouts. "I'm just finishing up. I'll be with you in a second!"

Jamie sat down near the door and readied her pad and pencil while Mr. Johnson's pedaling slowed to a halt.

"How've you been?" He asked, barely breathless or sweaty after his bout of strenuous activity.

"Anxious," Jamie smiled. "I'm learning that I have some serious changes to make in how I write if I want to be more successful at it."

Mr. Johnson nodded. "Good. You're learning important things about yourself—that in itself will help you. And let's see if we can do something about that anxiety." He took the chair next to Jamie's. "Do you remember where we left off last week?"

Jamie flipped to her notes. "Well, we worked on managing anxiety, first, by changing our perception of it. We talked about anxiety as an energizing force—a form of intensity that we can use to our advantage." Jamie looked up. Something was troubling her.

"Mr. Johnson, " she said frankly, "I've read over the notes, and understand that *intensity* is a more positive way to describe anxiety. But I still don't get how, exactly, it *helps* us on an exam."

"That's a good question, Jamie, " Mr. Johnson agreed. "Sports psychologists believe that in the right amount, intensity can actually boost performance. It affects our mind and body in so many ways. Physically, we may experience intensity in the form of greater strength and stamina. Our senses may seem sharper than ever. Mentally and emotionally, we may feel increased confidence and motivation to push ourselves to the limits of our performance.

"The point is, Jamie, if you think of your anxiety as intensity, you are already reframing it in a more useful light. You are developing a positive relationship with it. The next step is to explore ways to adjust your level of intensity so it works for you, rather than against you during the exam. In fact, that can be our goal for today's meeting."

Jamie nodded.

"First, let's build on what you are learning during your visits to Mrs. Flaherty. She told me that you are breaking down the task of writing an essay into small, manageable pieces."

"If I know the small things I can do to get started on my essay, I'll be less anxious." Jamie wondered if Mr. Johnson, too, was going to quiz her about GEARS.

Instead, he again turned the conversation to sports. "Do you know Craig Keller, the sprinter from our school who won two events at last year's Penn Relays?"

"You mean the guy who doesn't have to worry about SAT scores because he is already being recruited by the top schools in the country?"

"Yeah. That's the one." Mr. Johnson chuckled. "When Craig was a freshman, he joined the track team for the first time in his life. At that point, his running was pretty mediocre. But he had a lot of drive. And determination. He knew if he was going to someday race at a competitive level, he would have to shave at least three seconds off his time.

"Now three seconds in a sprint is like eternity. So to make the challenge more doable, Craig did some math."

"Some math?" Jamie wondered what math had to do with running a race.

"Some math," Mr. Johnson repeated. "He gave himself two years to improve his time. But he never said to himself, 'I have to improve my time by three seconds.' Instead, he divided three seconds by the number of weeks in two years. Then, he could say to himself, 'I have to improve my time by $6/1000^{th}$ of a second each week.' Of course, a reduction of $6/1000^{th}$ of a second per week is a more realistic and attainable goal than a reduction of a whole three seconds.

"So dividing the essay task into a series of smaller steps or activities towards the final result is the same idea. Instead of saying, 'I have to do a lot better at my writing,' and making yourself anxious at the size of the task, you can say, 'This week, I am going to work on understanding the goal of my essay. Next week I'll think about the kinds of experiences and examples I can use in my response. The week after that, I'll focus on the strategy it takes to develop my argument.' And so on. Breaking it down into smaller steps like this will make the entire project of writing an essay more manageable. With each step you master and begin to perform automatically, you will shave seconds or minutes off your time."

"Hmmm," Jamie thought aloud. "Mrs. Flaherty also showed me that the overall writing process can be broken down into four major steps or tasks—collecting information, planning, translating, and revising. She talked about *'Think to write'* and *'Write to think.'* Ten *more* steps to guide how and what I write. You were just talking about *one* of those steps—the *h* in *think*. It stands for *Hopping into GEARS,* or dividing the planning part of the writing process into yet *another* five smaller steps.

"Yup. I'm anxious, all right," Jamie said with a slight edge in her voice. "We're talking about a lot of steps here, Mr. Johnson. Maybe you can see why I'm feeling overwhelmed. It's gonna take a lot of practice first, to *remember* the steps and second, to do them automatically. Right now, it's hard for me to believe that one day all of these steps will come naturally when I write."

"Funny," Mr. Johnson replied. "This conversation reminds me of a headline I saw in the paper this morning, 'How to clean your house in nineteen minutes'—before you even leave for work. Thinking that this was an impossible feat, I read on. The author—one of those efficiency experts—broke the house down into the kitchen, living room, dining room and bedroom areas. Sure enough, she listed tiny, manageable tasks to do in these rooms that would each take seconds or a couple of minutes at the most to complete. If she had headed her story, 'forty-two things you can do to clean your house before you even get out the door in the morning,' most people would have felt immediately overwhelmed and turned the page.

"And she mentioned," he continued, "that the satisfaction you'd get from finishing one task, like feeling good about your clean and shiny kitchen sink, would spur you on to the next cleaning task."

Mr. Johnson smiled. "I was amazed. If I followed her advice and practiced her routine every morning, it would be a habit and my apartment would look super! Of course, I could alter the routine if I needed to, like when I have to clean for overnight guests and am forced to vacuum under the cushions of the sofa bed. Or unclog the shower drain.

"You are doing the same with your writing process, Jamie. To save time in the long run and help yourself get started and take control, you are making some of the smaller, basic writing tasks automatic. And the satisfaction you feel from accomplishing one small task will inspire you to move on to the next one.

"So before you leave today," Mr. Johnson promised, " I'll introduce you to some quick simple activities to help you manage your anxiety physically and mentally—tasks you can practice for a few minutes each day. I've taught other students, too, these activities, and would love to invite a couple over," he said, nodding his head in the direction of the exercise room, "so they can join us in our practice."

"Sounds good!" Jamie smiled and tried to sound as self-assured as Mr. Johnson. The voice inside her head saying, *'Great! More small steps to remember!'* faded to a whisper. Even though Jamie knew she was faking it, she was surprised at how pretending to sound confident actually made her *feel* more confident and helped to silence her voice of doubt. She watched as Mr. Johnson invited more students to join them.

"It's interesting," Mr. Johnson said as 3 more students pulled up their chairs by him and Jamie. "Before I started to consider anxiety as a positive form of energy, I used to think that showing athletes techniques to reduce their anxiety was enough to help their performance. For example, if you learn to breathe in a way that relaxes your mind and body, how can you feel anxious? If you are completely calm, cool, and collected before an event, won't that improve your performance? But I've learned over the years that deep breathing and progressive relaxation may not be enough.

"For some people, it can actually do more harm than good. If I were a Tsumai wrestler, I would want to be as pumped up as possible before my big match. A strong degree of intensity would be essential to face my opponent. Not overwhelming amounts of intensity, of course. But the right amount—which varies from person to person and depends on the situation—may actually help me perform at my best."

"So what do we do to feel that 'right' amount of intensity but not go over the line into anxiety?" Jamie asked.

"Well, I think you know the first part of that answer. Something your grandmother could have told you. To have the strength to manage your intensity, it is important to eat the right foods and get a good night's sleep—especially the night before the exam. When your body is well rested and nourished—when it is operating on a full tank of gas—it has an easier time responding to a stressful situation."

Jamie remembered the SAT essay didn't require the ancient student ritual of cramming the night before the exam, so she would have time to sleep—if she could. As for eating well—she would do her best to replace her usual Doritos with carrot sticks. But she knew there was more to it. "Okay. What else?"

"You could start by figuring out what the 'right' amount of intensity is for you. This means getting yourself into just the right frame of mind and mood to write. You can do this, but it takes some self-exploration and practice.

"Imagine that you are caught in a moment of feeling overwhelmed and distracted," Mr. Johnson explained. "That voice is screaming negative things at you inside your head. Your intensity turns to worry and self-doubt and prevents you from doing your best work. How can you crank down that intensity to a level that works for you? How can you transform distraction to concentration? Self-doubt to confidence? Negative self-talk to a positive inner voice? One that supports and encourages you? What does it take for you to enter just the right frame of mind and mood?"

"Are you asking us for the answer?" Jamie sounded surprised. "I thought you were going to tell *us* what to do, Mr. Johnson."

"The key is, you already know the answer. It is inside of you—somewhere in the back of your mind. Over the years you have collected images, feelings and sensations from the various experiences you've had in life. If I asked you to imagine yourself eating watermelon, running barefoot through cold mud, or forgetting everything you know during a test, I'm sure you could summon these experiences from the recesses of your mind.

"If you let your memory and imagination work freely, you could probably feel the wet sweet crunch of the watermelon, the cold, thick, brown mud oozing between your toes and sending shivers up your spine, or your heart racing from panic. Now, if we do a couple of exercises to help you relax, your imaginations might be able to work more freely and find the answers that you already hold inside."

Mr. Johnson rose from his chair and walked over to his desk. "So let's spend a few minutes discovering what works for you. First, I'm going to show you a couple of breathing and muscle relaxation techniques. And with your permission, I am going to tape our session so that all of you can listen, whenever you feel the need, to the techniques we are about to cover."

"Great," said Max, the star defender on the varsity soccer team.

Jamie shrugged, curious to begin and relieved that she no longer had to take notes. She shoved her pad and pencil back in her bag, and watched Mr. Johnson as he fumbled through the contents of his desk drawer. His hand finally emerged clutching an old-fashioned cassette tape and small recorder.

"I knew it was back there!" he exclaimed, and with one swift movement, popped the tape into the machine, placed it on the chair between them, and pressed the record buttons. No turning back now.

"By entering a relaxed state, you can explore your experience of intensity in a deeper, richer way. You can more fully sense what contributes to your intensity, and your power to control it. Also, knowing how to enter a relaxed state is itself a useful talent. It can help you to crank down the intensity when it reaches *too* high a level in other situations besides writing. Like before you have to give a class presentation."

Jamie was skeptical but intrigued. She knew the other athletes sitting with her had nothing but respect for Mr. Johnson and his "mental skills coaching." Maybe he could help her, too.

Mental Skills Coaching Part I: Exploring Your Intensity

"Sit," Mr. Johnson instructed, "with your feet firmly on the floor, and your back comfortably aligned against the back of the chair." He waited as they all shifted their postures and adjusted their feet, legs, and back into position.

"You can rest your hands above your knees," he continued, "then breathe slowly in and out—from your diaphragm rather than your chest. Just like a baby breathes while sleeping. You can see the baby's abdomen beneath the belly button rise and fall, up and down. As you breathe in through your nose, watch your own abdomen rise. As you breathe out through your mouth, watch your abdomen fall. That's it.

"This time, while you breathe in, count to three. Now hold that breath for a count of three, and exhale to a count of six. Then wait four seconds and start again. Like this. Inhale, 2, 3, hold, 2, 3, exhale, 2, 3, 4, 5, 6. Wait, 2, 3, 4. Inhale, that's right, hold, 2, 3, exhale, 2, 3, 4, 5, 6, wait, 2, 3, good! Inhale, 2, 3, hold, 2, 3, exhale, 2, 3, 4, 5, 6. Wait, ex-cel-lent! Inhale, 2, 3, hold, 2, 3, exhale, 2, 3, 4, 5, 6, wait, 2, 3, 4." Mr. Johnson spoke slowly, breathing along with his students.

"You can do this until you get a nice rhythm going and you feel your stomach below your belly button rise and fall. That's right. Keep counting to yourself. *Ex*cellent! Singers learn to breathe from their diaphragms. It helps them to control and project their voices, just as it can help you to control your level of intensity and project it into your writing."

Jamie felt the rhythm of her breathing in unison with the group. After five or six rounds, she could do it without counting, allowing her to concentrate more on Mr. Johnson's words.

"Now, as you continue to breathe, with each exhale, imagine the tension flowing out of your body. To imagine more clearly, you can close your eyes if you feel okay doing that. Good. Like water flowing from the faucet, imagine the tension draining out of you with each breath you exhale. Whatever thoughts enter your head, whatever worries or distractions—imagine them flowing into the stream of water and right out of your body.

"As you exhale, let the tensions drain out of your head, your neck and shoulders, right down through your arms, your fingers, and out your fingertips. Feel the heaviness as your muscles release the tension, as it slowly pours out of you and evaporates into a cloud, then into nothingness.

"Let the tension drip and then flow out of your back, washing down the front and back of your legs, your feet, and through your toes. Your legs may feel like limp rags as your muscles relax and let go of the tightness. Explore your body for any remaining tension or tightness, and as you exhale, let it go. That's it. When you are as comfortable and relaxed as you can possibly be, let me know by nodding your head."

After about a minute, Jamie slowly nodded.

"How do you feel right now?" Mr. Johnson asked.

"Totally relaxed. Not quite asleep, but almost. As if I am lying on a warm beach, soaking up the sun. I don't want to get up." The other students described similar feelings of relaxation, from drifting lazily in a rowboat to sitting atop a mountain in the fresh spring air.

"*Ex*cellent. Remember, anytime you want, you can recreate that sense of relaxation. This would be an ideal way to crank down the intensity when it gets to be too much. Practice breathing as I described, and let the tension drain out of you as you exhale.

"Visualize yourself on the beach, soaking up the rays," Mr. Johnson suggested. "Or imagine a place where you have felt calm, peaceful, and safe. What are the colors of that place? The sounds? The smells? As the image of this place becomes more vivid in your mind's eye—like you are watching it on a movie screen—the more relaxed you can feel in the present moment."

Jamie was mesmerized by the slow, deep rhythm of Mr. Johnson's voice.

As he paused, she continued to imagine the warm beach, the hot sand at her fingertips, the slight sting of the salty air on her cheeks and forehead, the smell of raw fish on the breeze. She could hear the gentle swish of the waves, and the tinkling of children's laughter in the distance. Just as Mr. Johnson described, a sensation of utter calm, peace, and safety enveloped Jamie like a soft blanket.

Mr. Johnson's voice seemed to float directly into her thoughts. "Just as your brain allows you to imagine a place of peace and safety, it can also allow you to float back to a time in your life when you were in just the right frame of mind and mood to perform your best. A time when you were feeling fully confident, focused, and absorbed in what you were doing, no matter how recently or long ago it occurred. Maybe it lasted just a brief moment, or several minutes, or even hours. Maybe people were around you, or your experience was a private one. Perhaps you were playing an instrument, or dancing on stage, or taking a test in your favorite subject. Or doing something else that brought out your best.

"You don't have to tell me anything about the experience if you don't want to. When your mind's eye sees a time that you felt you were performing at your peak, just nod your head."

"I can talk about it," Jamie volunteered first. Her eyes were closed as she explained, with a smile, "I was in the school play. I had the part of Corey Bratter in *Barefoot in the Park*. I felt like I was no longer Jamie on that stage but Corey, herself."

"Good. Now allow your brain to take you back through time to that performance. Just let yourself slip back to the time of the play and your transformation from Jamie into Corey Bratter. As you imagine that experience, you can begin to sense a return of those feelings of confidence and total absorption in what you are doing. You can notice how those feelings get stronger and stronger as you forget yourself and become the character of Corey onstage.

"And now, as you are enjoying those positive feelings, nod your head as they get stronger. That's right. Nod your head as a sign of your persuasive skills. Yes. You have convinced the audience that you are Corey Bratter. Just like you have forgotten Jamie, to make room for Corey Bratter, the people who are watching your performance have forgotten their own lives. They are on the edge of their seats, swept up in Corey's story. You have connected with your audience. Just continue to enjoy those feelings of connection. Of persuading others to believe in your performance. And the rest of you, too, can enjoy the sensations of performing your best, being in the zone."

As Jamie continued to nod her head, the positive feelings seemed to swell inside her.

"As you continue to enjoy your feelings, take a few deep breaths as we practiced before and allow the back of your mind to memorize all the wonderful sensations that you are experiencing—the natural endorphins that are released by your brain. In the future, whenever you nod your head like this during a performance, whether you are singing, playing a sport, writing, or doing another challenging activity, you will feel again these feelings of confidence and connection. You will experience the power of your persuasiveness, the sensation of forgetting yourself as you become completely absorbed in what you are doing. These feelings will flow through you and fill you as you nod your head."

Mr. Johnson paused, allowing Jamie and the group all the time they needed to memorize their feelings. "And now you can feel good about yourself, and confident that you have found a way to recapture these feelings whenever you need them.

"We are going to practice this a couple more times, and allow your brain to float back to other times when you performed your best, so your unconscious mind can memorize the feelings and store them as inner resources. You will be able to access these inner resources whenever you need them. Just nod your head, and the positive feelings will resurface for you. And the more you nod your head with conviction, the more vivid these feelings will be for you."

Mr. Johnson repeated the process two more times, asking the students to allow their brains to drift back to other moments of what he called "peak performances." By the third round, all they had to do was nod their head to summon the positive feelings that they associated with such moments. Jamie knew these feelings would help her face the task of writing a persuasive essay.

Mental Skills Coaching Part II—Bonus Exercise: Boosting your Confidence

When Mr. Johnson was confident that Jamie and the rest of them could access their positive feelings whenever they needed to, he asked Jamie to hang around for one more activity. An activity that would help boost her confidence during an exam or any moment of test anxiety.

"Maybe your mind will allow you to imagine one more thing. A time that you have been lost in your writing—a time that your ideas and thoughts were just flowing from your pen. A time when you had a clear sense of purpose and direction. When the ideas you needed to achieve your purpose and move in the right direction were bubbling at the surface. The right words came to mind without effort; they seemed to organize themselves in a logical, coherent way; the thoughts that were inside of you took shape in writing. The rest of the world disappeared—it was just you, your pen, your paper, and the words flowing from inside of you. I don't know if you felt this way recently, or you felt it a while ago. Whenever it happened, you felt the pure joy of expressing yourself without restraint. Whatever other people might think about what you were writing didn't matter. Writing was an easy, natural, and pleasurable experience."

Jamie closed her eyes again, remembering an experience five or six years ago in which her creative writing teacher had asked her to write a limerick. Although she had learned that limericks had particular requirements in terms of the number of lines, rhyme scheme, and rhythm, the rules of the task didn't slow her down. Just the right words and meter seemed to pour out of her.

She wrote about her pet turtle Frederick's attempted suicide one day as he dug a little too hard at the rock formation in his aquarium. A large rock, which had been poorly balanced on a smaller one, fell on top of him. Noticing his tiny tail jutting out from beneath the fallen boulder, Jamie saved him in the nick of time from being crushed to death. When she presented her rescue efforts in limerick form to the rest of the class, they roared with laughter.

Mr. Johnson's voice again penetrated her thoughts. "As you visualize yourself writing, see if you can imagine, on a scale of 1 to 10, with one being the lowest intensity and 10 being the highest intensity of all—the number that corresponds to the level of positive intensity that you feel when you are fully absorbed in your writing."

"Hmmm," Jamie replied. "When I am really into it, I feel a lot of positive intensity—probably a nine or a ten, and it is all channeled into my writing. Anything below a five would be too little, I think, to fully immerse myself in the task like I did. Yeah, I think about a nine or ten is right."

"Okay. A nine and a half, let's say. Now imagine yourself writing when you are distracted or perhaps overwhelmed by the task. You might want to recapture, for just a moment, what it felt like to write the SAT essay during your last exam experience—the one that caused you to feel panic. I don't want you to feel too uncomfortable right now, but allow just enough of the unpleasantness from that experience to come back, so that you can begin to feel some of those feelings of panic.

"On a scale of 1 to 10, how much of your intensity was negative? That is, how much of that intensity was a distracting force—preventing you from focusing on the writing task at hand? And how much of your intensity was positive? In other words, how much of that intensity fueled your writing process?"

"I would say that my positive intensity was only one or two, and my negative intensity was an eight or nine."

"Okay. Now I want you to have fun exploring something very interesting—a visualization technique that the psychologist Dr. Calvert Stein first introduced several years ago with people who wanted to feel more confident at what they were doing. I have adapted this technique to my writing and test taking. It helps me to transform my negative intensity into positive intensity so I have the energy I need to do my best.

"By clenching the fist of your non-dominant, or non-writing hand, you can transfer or displace these negative feelings—the ones that you rate at an eight or nine. Go ahead, Jamie, and close your left hand into a fist, and discover how all that negative intensity pours down your arm, into your hand, and comes to a standstill in your fist where you can hold it tightly in place. Allow the negative intensity—any unpleasant thoughts, emotions, and physical sensations—to gather from the different parts of your body and flow into your fist. Clench your fist hard, locking the negative intensity in your grasp, under your tight control. And when you feel that all, or most of that negative intensity is within your left fist's grasp, let me know."

Jamie could swear that she felt a stream of energy flow through the veins in her arms to her clenched fist. "Okay." She said to Mr. Johnson, when she visualized a concentrated mass of negative intensity sitting powerless, inside her curled fingers.

"Now, Jamie. You are the one in control. You are the one who transferred the negative intensity into your left fist, and you are the one who can decide, when you are ready, to replace that negative intensity with a positive, energizing force. I want you to discover how simple it is, to let those negative feelings go, and insert positive feelings in their place. When you are ready, you can nod your head, allowing those positive feelings that you experience during a time of peak performance, a time when you are at your best, to wash over you.

"As you nod your head, allow your brain to release endorphins and allow the positive feelings to spread inside of you. At the same time, allow your left hand to relax, loosening your fingers, letting the negative intensity flow from your grasp. That's right. Extend your fingers, shake them out, let the negative feelings evaporate. And maybe you'll observe that as you let go of the negative intensity, it is replaced by positive intensity. The more you nod your head in confidence, the more the negative intensity disappears into thin air and is replaced by positive sensations.

"When you feel the positive feelings build inside of you, and take on an energizing force, clench the fist of your dominant hand—so some of that positive intensity can concentrate in the hand that writes. And as you nod your head and clench your right fist, be aware of how you can project that positive intensity into the words that will flow from your pen. Discover how your fingers fill with the positive, energizing force as you write. This is the same intensity that fuels your thoughts, translates them to the written word, and connects you, through your writing, to others. And you can feel the pleasure of that positive intensity as you nod your head and tighten your fist in confidence.

"Spend a few moments sensing these pleasurable feelings, and take a few, relaxing breaths to help spread them throughout your body. You will be surprised by how these positive feelings will remain with you for a long, long time. At this moment, Jamie, how would you rate your intensity, both positive and negative, on a scale of 1 to 10?"

"My positive intensity would be at least a nine, and my negative intensity close to zero," Jamie replied without much thought.

"Great. You are a fast learner, Jamie. I know we've covered a lot of ground in a short period of time and you didn't have the chance to take notes. So let's summarize what we talked about.

"You now have a technique to control your intensity, and replace negative feelings with positive ones whenever you need to. Whenever you feel the negative intensity, just close your non-dominant or left fist. As you clench this fist, you will feel the negative feelings, thoughts and sensations flow into your tight grip. There, they will remain locked in your control. Once you feel that most or all of your negative intensity is securely trapped within your fist, you can replace the negative intensity with a positive force. All you have to do is nod your head, and allow the positive feelings and endorphins, summoned from your memories of peak performances, wash over you.

"As the positive feelings continue to grow inside of you, simply release your left fist, allowing the negative intensity to evaporate into nothingness. As you continue to nod your head, enjoy the positive intensity taking its place. As you enjoy these pleasurable sensations, clench your *right* hand, the hand that *writes*, into a fist. You will feel your positive intensity flow into this hand. Whenever you need it, you can project this intensity, this confidence, into your writing. And whenever you are ready, you can open your eyes... How do you feel?"

"I feel so good now, Mr. Johnson. Like I am floating on air. Thank you! Do you really think I can make myself feel this way again without your help?" Jamie asked, skeptical of her body's response and her new control of anxiety.

"Well, you *will* need my help. At first, that is. Here is the tape of our session." Mr. Johnson pressed the stop button, ejected the tape and passed it to Jamie. "I suggest that you listen to it at least once a day for as many days as you need to, and when you feel ready, put it away."

Jamie had all but forgotten about the recording. She felt reassured at the thought of being able to experience again what they had just covered. "Thanks again, Mr. Johnson."

Mr. Johnson nodded. At that moment, a group of muddy boys from the soccer team entered the training room. "Charlie rolled his ankle, again, Mr. Johnson," one of them moaned. "And our game against North is tomorrow."

Jamie slipped silently out the door.

That night, Jamie listened to her tape and once again experienced the positive energy flowing into her right hand. She went to bed in a good mood, savoring her feelings of confidence and control. She knew that with practice, by listening to the tape each day for the next few weeks, she could strengthen her ability to summon this energy during the SAT. Jamie switched off her bedside light, and for the first time since her parents' divorce—she felt comfortable in the darkness.

Chapter Seven

IDEATE: Ideas— Generate Some!

At their next meeting Mrs. Flaherty told Jamie, "You've inspired me to put together some worksheets on think!"

Jamie had to think a moment. "You mean the *think to write, write to think* think?" she asked.

"Yes. That think. I think we are up to the *i*," Mrs. Flaherty recalled. "Do you remember what the letters stand for?" Jamie's teacher was curious to know if her mnemonic strategy was working. Two weeks was the ultimate test of time.

"Mr. Johnson helped me with the *t—Transforming my mood*. And at our last session, you covered the *h* by showing me how to *Hop into GEARS*. *I* stands for *idiot*, I think. And *n* means *Narrate with* …something. *K* is *Keep your focus*."

Before Mrs. Flaherty had a chance to offer any corrections, Jamie pulled the *Think to Write—Write to Think* sheet from her folder and checked her answers. "Yesss! I nailed it!" she exclaimed, raising her fist high.

But then Jamie frowned. "I might remember what each letter stands for. That doesn't mean I know what the words *mean*, Mrs. Flaherty. Especially the word *idiot*. How does *idiot* apply to writing? Maybe how I felt the last time I wrote the SAT essay? Then I understand *idiot*."

"Eye-dee-ate, Jamie. *Ideate*, not *idiot*," and she wrote both words on the board so Jamie could see the spellings.

"You're right. We don't use the term *ideate* too often. At least not in everyday conversation," Mrs. Flaherty agreed. "But *ideate* comes from a word that you do know well: *idea*. So it just means to visualize or imagine; it means to create images in your mind's eye. When you plan your essay, you have to generate ideas, or *ideate* about your topic. Remember a couple of years ago when I taught your class about brainstorming? You were encouraged to generate freely as many different ideas as possible about the themes of your assignments. I asked you to allow your imaginations to take over."

"You mean when we made those webs?" Jamie recalled writing her topic in the middle of a page, circling it, and then quickly jotting down whatever popped into her head in association with the topic.

One day she won her class's respect for creating the largest, most intricate web ever. In mere minutes, Jamie conjured up over a hundred words and phrases in relation to the topic of *anger*. She remembered the satisfaction she had felt while circling in red each anger-laden word or phrase, and then drawing paths to connect the different words: annoyed, frustrated, missed the bus, pissed off, gained two seconds on my 100 fly, angry, fight with my mom, attack, rage, a big fat red *D* on my history test, explode, three days of lunchtime detention, and so on. Although her web ended up looking like ballooned dialogue from the pages of a comic book, Mrs. Flaherty had insisted on displaying it at the center of her bulletin board.

"Exactly." Mrs. Flaherty nodded. "Making a web is a process of ideating because it challenges you to generate ideas about a topic."

Jamie shook her head. "Webs take time, Mrs. Flaherty. I don't think I would be able to do one and write an essay both in twenty-five minutes."

Unless a teacher required her do draw a web first, Jamie was used to starting an assignment by just writing. She had realized after taking Mrs. Flaherty's writing assessment a couple of weeks ago that she hardly ever planned her essay. It just wasn't her habit, wasn't part of her writing process.

"I can understand how you think that twenty-five minutes is not enough," Mrs. Flaherty sympathized. "But remember, by hopping into GEARS first, you have already created the structure for your web—one that will guide your thinking and generation of ideas from the start. In fact, because this particular web will help provide the direction for your argument, I prefer to call it a map. A GEARS map. All you need to do is fill it in with your ideas."

Jamie shook her head. She still didn't understand how this map thing could help her to save time.

Mrs. Flaherty seemed to read her thoughts. "The key is, Jamie, the more experiences you map *before* taking the SAT, the more immediate ideas you'll have in response to the SAT writing prompt—whatever that prompt may be. In fact, you may already have a map in your head when you write the SAT essay. You may even have several maps in your head! Each time you map an experience, you force yourself to think about it at a deeper, more insightful level. Then you can use your insights to answer all sorts of writing prompts. We'll talk more about this at our next meeting. Before we can head in that direction, we have to make sure our *GEARS Map* is clear."

Mrs. Flaherty retrieved yet another worksheet from her file drawer and handed it to Jamie. Lines and circles covered the entire page. GEARS Map was printed in the upper left hand corner.

"Last time we met, we defined what each letter in the GEARS Map stands for..."

Jamie looked up, as if GEARS were written in the air above her head. This had been her homework. To memorize GEARS, to make the letters stick. She recited each one: "*G* stands for the *goal* of my essay—what I am trying to prove. *E* stands for the *example of experience*—the specific case I will use to prove my points. *A* stands for my *argument*, itself. *R* stands for the specific *reasons*, at least three, to back up my argument. And *S* stands for the *supporting evidence and details* that I can draw from my experience to prove my argument." Jamie was proud she could recall what each letter of GEARS meant, but she knew that to really understand the model, she would have to be able to come up with examples, too, for each letter. She didn't feel like she could do that yet.

Mrs. Flaherty was impressed for the second time that hour. "Excellent," she beamed. "Now you can create your GEARS map and use it as your guide in the actual test situation. And this is where you start."

Jamie heaved a sigh of relief as her teacher pointed to a box labeled *Essay Goal* in the upper-right hand corner of the handout. Thank goodness Mrs. Flaherty was going to give her the examples for each letter.

"It takes seconds to figure out the goal of your essay because the words for it are practically handed to you," Mrs. Flaherty explained. "You derive them directly from the essay prompt. You want to write a goal that captures, as precisely as possible, what the prompt is asking you to achieve. Remember my example, *"One step forward, two steps backwards?"*

Jamie nodded.

"I fill in my box: Goal -- to show that a step forward is followed by two steps backwards. Or," Mrs.Flaherty continued, "in my own words, *to show that a positive development may do more harm than good.* Another way to put it is *to show that progress may result in a setback.* Or, *to show that we may have to pay a price to advance."*

"Figuring out the goal doesn't even require much ideating or brainstorming," Mrs. Flaherty promised. "All I have to do is reread the prompt, decide if I agree and/or disagree with the statement, and find the words to express what it is that I want to show in my essay. Then I can fill in the goal on my GEARS Map. If it is a fill-in-the-blank prompt, my task is even easier. My goal is already laid out for me. I just have to insert in the blank the experience I choose to use as the basis for my argument."

"Once I've determined my goal, Jamie, the fun of ideation begins! I know the general direction that my essay is headed, but I still have to figure out the bends and turns along the way. My unconscious mind is a rich storehouse of information about experience. Like the boxes of supplies in a storehouse, it holds the examples and details I need to shape my argument. Just open the storehouse, reach into a box and grab some. By brainstorming, I can unlock my own storehouse and tap into the wealth of ideas my unconscious has contained for my essay.

"Keep in mind, Jamie, brainstorming about my experience comes easily to me because I have been doing it for so long. It is now an automatic part of my writing process. I can come up with a number of experiences in my own life or observations I have made of others' experiences to prove that progress may lead to setbacks. So I'll brainstorm aloud. See if you can follow my train of thought.

Jamie shifted forward in her seat, as if to brace herself for another ride in her grandfather's stick shift car. This time, they were headed into the GEARS Map.

"What could be considered positive developments—*steps forward*—but with a price?" Mrs. Flaherty wondered aloud. "Hmmm. Technological advances; after all, we tend to think of TV; the Internet; communication by email, cell phone; instant and text messaging; Palm Pilots; and so on as advances we cannot live without. Yet, horror stories abound about peoples' experiences with these technologies. Like my friend's husband who was in a tragic car accident when talking on his cell phone at a busy intersection. Or the 12-year-old girl who befriended a person on the Internet, thinking he was a nice kid her age. She ended up being stalked by a 58-year-old serial killer.

Jamie winced.

"Or, maybe," Mrs. Flaherty continued, " I'll think of personal steps forward that I, or someone else has made in life, but in the end, these developments caused greater harm than good. Like my grandmother who took some medication to help manage her depression, but suffered some uncomfortable side effects. Or my brother who signed a contract to play Division I basketball in college. He was looking forward to a promising career. A future that he hoped would include the NBA. But during his freshman year, a knee injury put a stop to it. He still has to deal with pain and trip after expensive trip to the doctor ten years later.

"Any or all of these experiences can be used to address the writing task. However, to prevent myself from taking on too much in twenty-five minutes, I am going to go with one, maybe two experiences only. In the end, if I stick with just one example of experience that I know well, digging deep for rich details on just that one experience, I will have plenty to write about. So I fill in the circle at the center of my GEARS Map:

Example/s of experience - <u>*TV or cell phones*</u>

Now that I've chosen the example of my experience, I will draw from that experience the reasons to support my argument. These reasons are what satisfy the question, *Why?* In other words, *why is a step forward followed by two steps backwards?*

"For example, if I choose TV as the step forward, I can brainstorm different ways that TV has helped my life, such as entertaining me while I fold baskets of laundry, bringing news of the outside world into my home, and showing me how other people live and deal with their problems. But TV is also a disruptive force in my family life. We constantly battle over who watches what when; TV violence causes my little nephew to have nightmares; and TV helps me avoid whatever I *should* be doing, like putting away the laundry, getting exercise, or correcting students' papers.

"If I choose cell phones as my experience, I can show how they are both helpful AND disruptive in peoples' lives. For example, cell phones can be a lifeline if my car breaks down on a deserted highway in the middle of the night, if I'm lost and need to call someone for directions, or if my son is stranded on a soccer field because we didn't see the email that his practice was cancelled; on the other hand, cell phones can be a nuisance when they ring during my class, play *Mission Impossible* in the middle of a our midterm exam, and, of course, when they distract drivers who end up going 30 miles per hour in the fast lane.

"In the end, I decide that I am going to limit myself to the example of TV. I realize that if I use the example of cell phones as well, I might be trying to squeeze in too much within a twenty-five-minute time frame. So I resolve that less is more. Now I am ready to fill in at least three circles on my GEARS Map with reasons that TV, although a step forward, can have negative effects:

Reasons—
1. TV violence can have a negative influence on kids
2. TV can disrupt family life
3. TV can distract me from focusing on more important things in my life

In fact, if I look at my three reasons, I have the makings of a *thesis*; that is, a yet-to-be-proven statement that I present as the premise of my argument, the position I will defend throughout my essay. It contains the line of reasoning behind my argument. For example, I can state, "TV enables us to connect with the vast world beyond our family room. But we pay a dear price for this connection. *The disruptive influences that TV has had on my home and work life may, at times, outweigh the benefits.*"

Jamie was listening closely to Mrs. Flaherty's stream of thought. "That sounds like it would be a good argument," she agreed. "Are you saying, though, that I have to fill in my reasons before I can fill in my argument?" Studying her GEARS Map, Jamie had noticed that Mrs. Flaherty seemed to skip over the *A* in *GEARS* altogether.

"That's a good question, Jamie. My answer is, 'it depends.' You can complete your GEARS Map according to the way your brain works. Some people seem to immediately have an argument—without much prior brainstorming. Perhaps they have already given their experience a great deal of thought and the position they choose to argue in their essay comes to them automatically. We mentioned this a few weeks ago when we talked about the kind of essay that the SAT challenges you to write—a persuasive one. Your argument may already be bubbling at your mind's surface because you've previously considered it from several angles. That debate that you had on lowering the minimum drinking age from 21 to 18, for example, contains the seeds of a persuasive essay.

"On the other hand, the prompt may present you with a completely new idea. Let's say you've never really thought before about the line from Kenny Rogers' song, *The Gambler:* 'You've got to know when to hold them, know when to fold them....'" Mrs. Flaherty sang off-key. "You might agree with this statement after playing several games of Texas Hold'em, but you still need to figure out the reasons why this statement holds true in other situations. Maybe you have experienced or observed some situations that just got too risky.

"Like my friend who rented her mother's old house to someone who seemed like a nice, respectable guy. He paid his rent on time. When things broke down, he insisted on fixing them himself. My friend never had to call a plumber or electrician. And best of all, he took loving care of her mother's garden. But when she discovered marijuana plants in the basement, she realized it was time to 'fold them.' Time to turn him in and find a new tenant.

"By the same token, the prompt might be the fill-in-the-blank-with-your-choice-of-an-experience type, such as, *If I had the authority to choose the next President of the United States, I would choose....*' For the first time in your life, you consider the possibility of Jimmy Black, the rap singer, for President. Because you have never thought about this idea before, you must come up with the reasons for your choice without much forethought. You must think from scratch.

"Yet another group of people may prefer to start out by brainstorming the particulars of their experience even before they know their argument or the reasons to support it. Think of the investigators on one of those TV crime shows. Have you noticed how they often recreate the scene of the crime based on just a few strands of evidence?"

Jamie nodded. "I love those shows. The characters manage to come up with an elaborate explanation for what happened by the end of the program, even though they barely have a single clue to start out with.

"Are you saying, Mrs. Flaherty, that once I've chosen an example of experience, I can jump all the way to the s in GEARS—the *supporting evidence and details*—and work my way backwards? Shouldn't GEARS be GESRA, then, instead?"

"It depends on the information you have at the beginning of your process," Mrs. Flaherty replied. "Like Sherlock Holmes, you might prefer to use a very common form of what is called inductive reasoning. From the evidence you have uncovered, you could propose a solution to the case. Our brains may work the same way to form an argument. We build our reasons and arguments from the details—or evidence—of our experience. Some people call this 'working backwards' to a thesis. A web or GEARS Map enables us to picture these details and the ways they connect with one another; in other words, the map shows us the paths back to our conclusions or argument.

"If we extend the map metaphor, the themes of these connections become the reasons in our argument. For example, I can remember the numerous fights I had with my parents and siblings over who got to watch their TV show, and the times I had to stay up late to finish my schoolwork because I got sucked into a TV program. I turned into a useless zombie.

"Even today. Why do they have to show *Desperate Housewives* and so many fun sitcoms on Sunday night? The night before my lesson plans are due? So I can come up with at least one answer to the question, 'why is tele-

IDEATE: Ideas—Gener*ate* Some! 77

vision sometimes a setback in my life?' Because it has a disruptive influence on *both* my family life and work."

Jamie studied her map. "Okay. So I understand the little circles labeled supporting evidence and details, and I see how they feed into the main reasons for your argument." She traced the lines with her fingers. "But I don't get the circles that are sprouting from the example of experience in the center. They aren't connected to the reasons, but you've labeled them as supporting background details."

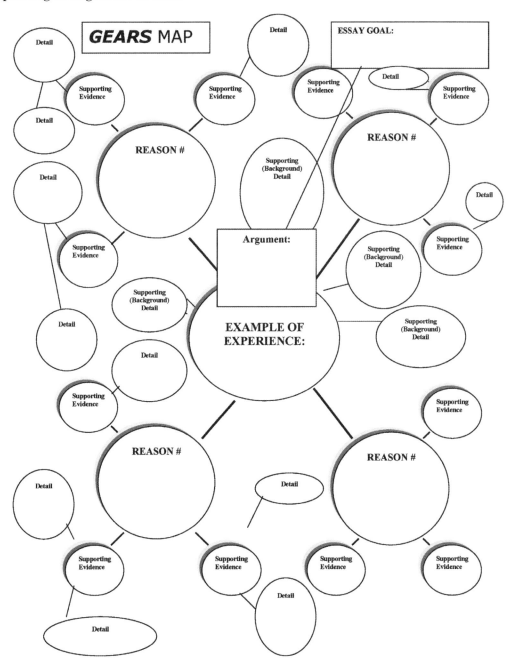

"Quite often, Jamie, before you launch your argument, you need to supply your reader with some background about your experience. These details should help you set the stage for your argument; for example, I might want to explain to my reader what is positive about my TV example before I show the negatives. Or, maybe I need to define my terms and example of experience more specifically. Am I referring to any special kind of TV, like reality shows or Monday Night Football? Or am I thinking of a particular channel like the Discovery Channel, the History Channel, or the Walt Disney Channel? Am I talking about any specific length of time for watching TV, like four hours a day or two hours a night? Whatever my topic, I need to present those few background details which are necessary for the reader to understand my argument."

"What if I decided to write about my parents' divorce?" Jamie asked. "Would I have to present all the background details about their breakup?"

"No. You select only those details that are necessary for the reader to grasp your line of reasoning," Mrs. Flaherty replied. "If your argument is that over time, divorce leads to stronger family ties, then the reader might benefit from knowing how long your parents have been apart. But," she cautioned, "you don't want to present *too* many background details, because then you run the risk of going off track with your essay, getting bogged down in the details. Remember, you have limited time to persuade your readers. You want to move forward to your argument, to proving your main points."

Jamie continued to study her worksheet.

"Why not fill out one of these maps?" Mrs. Flaherty suggested. "Notice that the first sheet is a key to the GEARS Map, and then two more versions besides the one with circles. Each map gives you a different way to present your goal, example of experience, argument, reasons, and supporting details.

"If you like to go where the spirit leads you, the circular style is for you. If you think in a more linear way, that is, you love outlines that show the order and sequence of your ideas, step one leads to step two leads to step three and so on, then the second or third map might work better for you. The second map is presented in a structured table format and the third map is arranged like an organizational chart.

"Try them all! Decide which kind of map helps you to brainstorm the most effectively—chances are your mind prefers to use one kind of map over the other. Once you've selected a map type, see how far your ideas take you. Fill up the page as quickly as you can."

Mrs. Flaherty glanced at her watch and winced. "We'll have to meet again next week at the same time and talk about it, Jamie. I have a couple more important points to make about ideation before we move on to the n in *think*. But what I have to say won't make much sense until you do your own GEARS Map."

"Okay, Mrs. Flaherty." Jamie grinned. She remembered how much fun it had been to map her anger over her parents' divorce two years ago. Now she was in a different place. She had some new ideas to generate about life after divorce. Like her mother's reawakening. Jamie's mom could do things that before had been Dad's job. Like ushering the fruit bats out of the attic bedroom. Or lying flat on her back under the car to change the oil filter.

"Oh, and one more thing before you go," Mrs. Flaherty remembered. "Do something to lift your spirits before you brainstorm. To get yourself into a positive mood. Run a couple of miles in the park. Play your favorite music. Watch an uplifting movie scene. Practice what Mr. Johnson has been teaching you to transform your mood. I just read an article in the newspaper about how a positive mood actually helps the creative process, especially the generation of ideas."

"Thanks, Mrs. Flaherty. Wish me luck! First I'm going shopping at the mall to put myself in a good mood. Then I'll go home and … what's that word? Oh yeah! Ideate!" Jamie left the classroom still clutching her GEARS Map.

KEY TO THE GEARS MAP

Goal – What the essay assignment or question instructs you to do; the specific task you are prompted to address in the essay assignment.
In this essay assignment, I am asked to agree or disagree with the statement, "Behind every cloud there is a silver lining." Since I agree with this statement, my goal is to show or argue that every cloud has a silver lining – meaning that something positive can come out of something negative.

Example/s of Experience – What has happened or is happening in your life, someone else's life, or in the world that contains the evidence to achieve your essay's goal; an event or set of events that you have studied, read about, personally encountered, or observed from which you can draw the evidence and details to support your case or argument and address the essay task.
The experience from which I will draw the evidence and supporting details to develop my argument, "Every cloud has a silver lining," is my parents' divorce.

Argument – Your position or point of view, and the line of reasoning behind it. In concise form, your argument becomes the thesis statement.
Through <u>my parents' divorce</u>, I learned that every obstacle can be an opportunity because the divorce <u>gave me the chance to grow closer to my brother</u>, <u>discover dimensions of my parents that I never knew existed</u>, and <u>take on new roles and responsibilities in the family</u>.

Reasons – The statements that drive your central argument. These statements are included in your argument and answer the question, *"Why?"* They represent the conclusions or insights you have gained from thinking deeply about your example of experience. They are introduced in your argument, and then become the main ideas you develop to achieve the goal of your essay.

Behind every cloud is a silver lining. Or, something positive can result from something negative. Why?

Reasons: *My parents' divorce was, at first, like a storm cloud that had hit my life. But...*
1. Through my parents' divorce, I grew closer to my brother John.
2. After my parents' divorce, my family grew and I developed new relationships.
3. Because of my parents' divorce, I took on new roles and responsibilities in the family.
4. After the divorce, I discovered some positive changes in my parents.

Supporting evidence and details – the *specific* facts, illustrations/sensory description, comparisons/contrasts, explanations or elaborations, necessary background information about your experience, quotes or expert opinions, actions, dialogue, and inner thoughts that lead to the reasons behind your argument.
I saw my Dad cry; My mom fixed the toilet herself; John threw the lacrosse ball around with me; I felt shock, disbelief and denial when my mother told me about the divorce.

IDEATE: Ideas—Generate Some!

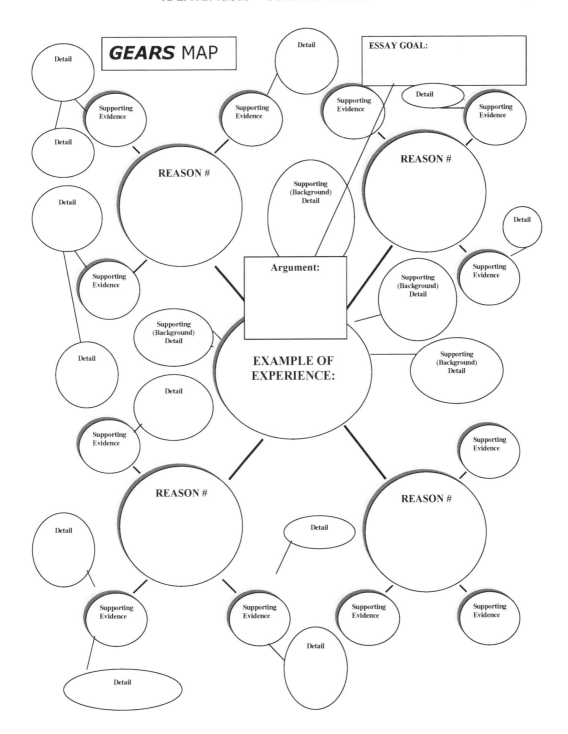

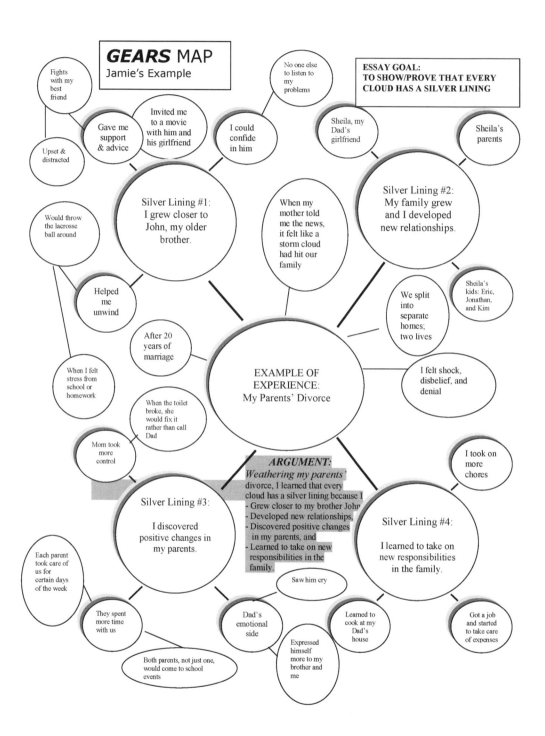

HOPPING INTO GEAR/S

GOAL: TO SHOW/PROVE THAT EVERY CLOUD HAS A SILVER LINING

Experience: My parents' divorce

Supporting Background Details:
- When my mother told me the news, it felt like a storm cloud had hit our family
- After 20 years of marriage
- We split into separate homes; two lives
- I felt shock, disbelief, and denial

Argument: Weathering my parents' divorce, I learned that every cloud has a silver lining because I 1) grew closer to my brother John, 2) learned to take on new responsibilities in the family; and 3) discovered positive changes in my parents.

Reason #1 I grew closer to John, my older brother.	*Reason #2* I learned to take on new responsibilities in the family.	*Reason #3* I discovered positive changes in my parents.
Supporting Evidence and Details: 1.1. Gave me support & advice when I was fighting with my best friend 1.2. When I felt stress from school or homework, he would throw the lacrosse ball around with me and help me unwind 1.3. Invited me to go to a movie with him and his girlfriend	**Supporting Evidence and Details:** 2.1. Learned to cook at my Dad's house 2.2. Got a job and started to take care of my own expenses 2.3. I took on more chores	**Supporting Evidence and Details:** 3.1. Each parent took care of us for certain days of the week; they spent more time with us. Both parents, not just one, would come to school events. 3.2. We saw Dad's emotional side. He expressed himself more to my brother and me. I saw him cry for the first time. 3.3. Mom took more control of things. When the toilet broke, she would fix it rather than call Dad.

HOPPING INTO GEAR/S

GOAL: To show …

Experience:

Supporting Background Details:

Argument:

Reason #1

Reason #2

Reason #3

Supporting Evidence and Details:

1.1._____

1.2._____

1.3._____

Supporting Evidence and Details:

2.1._____

2.2._____

2.3._____

Supporting Evidence and Details:

3.1._____

3.2._____

3.3._____

Chapter Eight

Narrate with Insight

Nothing ever becomes real till it is experienced. Even a proverb is no proverb to you till your life has illustrated it. —John Keats

Mrs. Flaherty stood on the chair, straining to insert a disc into the DVD player suspended from the classroom ceiling.

"There," she huffed, pressing the play button in triumph. "Jamie, I want you to watch this. It'll set the stage for us to talk about the *n* in think—*narrate with insight.*"

Mrs. Flaherty jumped down from her perch, her eyes glued to the scene unfolding on the TV monitor:

"Just one last question. Can I ask you, Billy, what does it *feel* like to dance?"

"Dunno," replied the eleven-year-old star of the film, *Billy Elliot.*

Jamie couldn't believe her eyes. She had just rented this movie last month, after arriving at the video store too late to find any new releases. Amanda, her ballet-obsessed friend, was the one who found *Billy Elliot* hiding in the rows of foreign dramas.

On the screen above, a panel of admissions officers shook their heads, ready to close Billy's file. Jamie remembered the boy's fragile situation. Other than an enthusiastic letter of recommendation from his ballet teacher, he had little to support his application to London's premier dance academy. The school physician had detected a "tiny curve" in his spine. After an awkward audition of ungraceful moves, the judges were more befuddled than impressed by Billy's talent. To add to the strikes against him, Billy had punched another hopeful applicant (that afternoon) in the locker room. So the committee offered Billy one last question—one last chance to make a more favorable impression.

At first, Billy stood in painful silence. But slowly, he started to speak and his voice gained strength. Soon his stiffness and anxiety disappeared. "Once I get going I forget everything... I can feel a change in my whole body...."

While Billy described what he felt like dancing, his eyes—which before had been filled with frustration—seemed to soften with a wisdom beyond his years: "I'm just there flying like a bird. Like electricity…."

Maybe the judges had once been dancers and on some level, Billy's words stirred their own raw sensations of the dance experience. Touched by his insightful answer, they were ready to view Billy's candidacy in a new light.

Mrs. Flaherty mounted the chair once again, this time to eject the DVD from its slot. "I wanted you to watch this scene, Jamie, because it shows what happens in the process of finding the words to tell or *narrate* your story. It shows what might occur to you as you brainstorm about or immerse your self fully in an experience and grasp or intuit the core meaning. It shows *insight*. It shows that Billy intuits the nature of dance. He 'gets it.'"

"Insight?" Jamie repeated the word.

"Yes, "replied Mrs. Flaherty. "Just as Billy's insightful response had a positive, maybe even profound impact on his judges, the SAT essay that gets the highest score is the one written with 'insight'– a process that calls upon our ability to intuit the true or inner nature of things.

"Billy had intuited the inner nature of dance and then, at that moment, found the words to capture his insight and show the admissions committee his passion was genuine. In the same way, when we write with insight, we find the words to grasp the very core of human experience and connect with our readers on a deeper level. We write with our hearts in mind."

Jamie tried to soak in Mrs. Flaherty's explanation. What exactly did *intuit* mean? She was relieved to see her teacher reaching towards the drawer. Some examples of insight from the monster files would be helpful.

"Read this, Jamie." Sure enough, Mrs. Flaherty emerged with a handout entitled *Narrate with Insight* to illustrate her point. "Kelsey Johnson, a high school junior, creates this kind of insightful connection with her 'audience' in her essay about *strength in numbers*."

Jamie read:

We scurried around the wet, slippery deck, grabbing onto each other as one of us started to slip toward the leeward side of the boat. Rule number one: Always look out for your shipmates ahead of yourself. There is no room for selfishness. It is a rare and comforting feeling knowing that you have seven people around you who are willing to risk their lives to protect yours...

We frantically ran around trimming sails that flapped violently in the wind, tacking with the frequent wind changes, and reefing the mainsail when the wind became too strong. We worked so well together no one even needed to speak, except for the occasional, "Be careful." We all knew what to do, but even the most basic sail handling could turn into a life-or-death situation in the intensity of the storm.

I loved every minute of it.

Insight and Experience

"You see, Jamie," Mrs. Flaherty explained, "As Billy Elliot and Kelsey reveal, insight reflects their inner sense of a situation. This achievement of insight is also considered an important sign of our ability to make sense out of *emotional* experiences—to understand the heart of a matter."

Jamie struggled to reign in her wandering thoughts. Not long ago, she had been forced to make sense of her own emotional experience. She was sent to the guidance counselor for lashing out in anger at every teacher, administrator, or fellow student who crossed her path. Although at first she had been unaware of what triggered her outbursts, the counselor listened patiently while Jamie sorted through a tangled web of thoughts and feelings. It took her almost a year of visits to realize that the anger granted her a momentary sense of power and control. In fact, it helped to mask other uncomfortable feelings that she was experiencing because of situations that were *out* of her control, such as her sadness over the death of a cousin. Not to mention the constant stream of disappointment, frustration, anxiety, pain, self-pity, resentment, and so on, which sprang from her parents' divorce.

Jamie was so lost in her thoughts that she failed to notice the new essay on her lap. "Do you remember this one?" Mrs. Flaherty was asking.

"Oh." Jamie glanced at the strangely familiar title, "Anger Builds Character," and read:

At first, I believed that everyone was the enemy. It was their fault my best friend was avoiding me; it was because of them that I felt so abandoned, so betrayed. The day that I ran out of reasons to feel sorry for myself was the day that the truth finally penetrated. The only enemy I had to face was the one inside of me.

"This is mine," Jamie whispered. Mrs. Flaherty had saved her essay inside the *Narrate with Insight* file.

Insight and Sudden Awareness

"That's right, Jamie. I will always keep this essay. It shows that in addition to the meaning we make of our emotional experiences, insight is what happens in the moment when we see things in a new light; after being stuck, we suddenly figure out a way to solve the problem or meet the challenge. We might experience a flash of understanding or intuition or a sudden shift in perspective—an 'aha' or 'click' of instant awareness.

"Maybe we stumble upon a strategy to bend the rules without breaking them or to approach a situation from 'outside the box.' Or, maybe we discover another, even kinder method to trap a mouse."

Mrs. Flaherty handed Jamie yet another essay from the deep *Insight* file. "All it takes to capture this sudden awareness, Jamie, is a couple of words, sentences, or even paragraphs. Consider, for example, Jason Ritchie's response to the statement, *"People learn more from their shortcomings than from their strengths."*

I used to think that losing the season basketball title was the end of the world. But in one fleeting moment, after falling in the semifinal championship game to our uptown arch rivals, I learned that losing doesn't break you, it makes you.

The writer went on to describe his "fleeting moment" of insight –

I walked off the court towards the locker room, eying the rows upon rows of victory banners that lined the far wall of the gym. I was once struck by how they dated all the way back to 1952. The large gaps between the years were amusing. Sometimes ten, sometimes fifteen—even twenty years would go by before my school won another conference title in any sport. But in spite of those enormous gaps in time between championships, the rows of banners hung in perfect succession. 1952, 1957, 1961, 1969, and so on. Not one line was broken.

Suddenly, I knew that our loss did not interrupt the flow of victory. Our school's team would regroup and reform until it hit another winning combination—maybe next year, the year after, or even ten years down the road. Without the banner to show for it, my team would still leave its mark. What we gained from our defeat would make the next victory banner possible. I realized that like a good book, the part that is left out—what happens "between the lines"—might be the most important chapter of all.

Jamie couldn't believe that a high school student had written these words.

Mrs. Flaherty seemed to read her thoughts. "I am often amazed at the maturity and wisdom that students convey in their essays. I guess that narrating with insight is often a process of self-discovery. Meaning you don't know the insightful idea ahead of time. But writing forces you to sort through your thoughts and ideas about an experience, and discover what it means to you.

"And isn't self-discovery a rite of passage at your age? Aren't teenagers famous for questioning rules and authority? For questioning themselves? In other words, now is the time to let your natural tendency toward rebellion, self-doubt, learning, personal growth, and creativity go wild. Now is the time to reveal your capacity to intuit the heart of a situation, challenge the way things are, draw lessons from experience, and look at the world from a totally different angle!"

Jamie nodded, amused, but at that moment unable to capture Mrs. Flaherty's enthusiasm. She knew from experience that being insightful was not easy. "I wrote with insight once, but how do I do it again in twenty-five minutes, on command? It took me almost a year to achieve the insight I wrote in my *Anger Builds Character* essay."

"You are asking me about a *process*, Jamie -- one that leads to moments of intuition, deep understanding, or sudden awareness. You are right. I can't guarantee that you will go through this process while writing the SAT essay. But I can guarantee that at the very least, you can draw from previous experiences of achieving insight. Even before you walk into the exam room, you are full of insights. These are the lessons you have learned from a whole lifetime of experience."

Jamie's eyes spelled doubt.

"Trust me. A closer look at writing as an act of learning will provide us with some insights about the insight process."

Insight and The Learning Cycle

Mrs. Flaherty continued her explanation. "Very few activities enable us to both achieve and show insight at the same time. Writing is one of these activities. As we write, a unique phenomenon occurs. We take in the outer world, and find the words to bring out our inner world. David Kolb, a psychologist, refers to this process of bringing the outside in and the inside out as 'the learning cycle.'

"Picture, for example, the case of Justin—a typical high school senior. Sarah, a close friend gives Justin a CD for his birthday. Justin has never heard of the artist who recorded the CD, but Sarah explains, 'When I listened to this, I thought of you.'

"As Justin pops the new release into the CD player, he is instantly swept away. The first song reminds him of playing Frisbee on a golden beach with turquoise waves licking his toes. Justin nods in approval, and later puts the CD in his favorite storage rack—the one with the music he plays to help him unwind after a long day.

"By trying out the new CD, Justin has unwittingly experienced the learning cycle. First came the *experience* that he took in from the outside world—Sarah's gift of unfamiliar music. Listening to the new songs. Next came the *processing* of the experience: as Justin listened to the CD, he had pleasurable thoughts and feelings in association with it. Then he drew a *conclusion* from his experience: Sarah was right—he loved this music, and would certainly *apply* his new insight. The next time he needed to relieve some stress, this was the CD he would pick to help him relax.

"Justin's music, Billy Elliot's dance, Kelsey's storm at sea, your anger, and Jason's observation of the line of victory banners are the experiences that set the stage for the learning cycle: first, taking in or reliving the *experience*; second, *processing* or sorting through different thoughts and feelings about the experience; then, forming *ideas, conclusions* or *generalizations* about the experience; and finally, *applying* what has been learned to daily life. In this cycle of experiencing, processing, generalizing and applying, you all gained insights to enrich your own and others' lives."

Applying the Learning Cycle to the SAT Essay

"So, in response to your earlier question, Jamie—yes, you have the capacity to show insight in twenty-five minutes or less. In fact, as we discussed in our first meeting, every student taking the SAT brings a lifetime of experience to the test situation. Although you cannot choose the SAT assignment, you can choose a meaningful experience—whether a personal memory, a favorite literary figure with whom you connect, or even a historical event—to provide the basis for your insights. As long as you have an experience, you can begin the cycle of learning that leads to insight."

"Where does the GEARS Map fit in?" Jamie asked.

As usual, Mrs. Flaherty had an answer in her files. She reached into the back of her drawer and pulled out a map and an essay without even flipping through any of the alphabetized folders. Jamie wondered how Mrs. Flaherty could possibly know the precise location of each paper she had saved over the years.

"Here, Jamie. Sandra Guirguis, a high school junior, wrote an essay in response to the statement, 'Suffering builds character.' Using the learning cycle as a guide, she chose a recent experience in which she had undergone reconstructive surgery for a torn ligament in her knee—an injury that would cause her to miss an entire year of varsity soccer. To immerse herself and her reader in the first two phases of the learning cycle, *experiencing* and *processing,* she used her GEAR/S Map. Take a look."

Jamie saw that Sandra had captured several details of her experience on the map, including the words of the conversation that she had with her mother right before the ACL surgery, her description of the drain sticking out of her knee after the operation, and the throbbing pain that she felt in the first few days of recovery. Sandra also brainstormed about what she had learned from Roy Hobbs, the main character in *The Natural*, the novel she read during her recovery.

Jamie glanced at the essay attached to the web:

She clenched my hand, nearly cutting off my circulation.

"I love you," she whispered.

"Mom, it's just knee surgery," I assured her, "I'll be out of here in a couple of hours."

My ACL reconstruction went smoothly. The next thing I knew, I was at home covered by my light blue comforter with a big brace and drain sticking out of my knee. My knee burned. It felt as if it had its own heartbeat, pulsating rapidly like it had just run the marathon. I scanned my room in hopes of finding something to distract me from the pain. At the end of my bed my mom had left me a pile of books. I struggled to grab one, and picked up The Natural, *by Bernard Malamud.*

As I read, Roy Hobbs, the main character, became my new companion. I almost forgot about the surging pain in my knee. I listened as Roy promised that he was going to become the greatest baseball player there ever was. Then it happened. This strong and invincible character was struck down by a bullet. His dreams were shattered. I felt a lump in my throat. I remembered when my knee shattered, and with it, what felt like the shattering of my athletic career...

"That's how I felt when my parents divorced!" Jamie exclaimed, "Like my whole life had been shattered."

"Yes! When you share your insights like Sandra does in this essay, you are connecting on some level with your reader. After all, as long as we are human, we have the capacity to relive our memories and emotions and become absorbed in our own and others' experience. Billy Elliott connected with the admissions committee by communicating what it feels like to dance. Sandra captures how it feels to lose what seems like a part of her identity—an insight that touches upon your own sense of loss, Jamie, at the divorce of your mom and dad. When we narrate with insight, we more deeply engage our readers and draw them right through the learning cycle with us. No wonder the College Board says that insight is the mark of a high-scoring SAT essay."

"So *ideation*, then, is what helps us to achieve insight?" Jamie asked, once again trying to tie in the *think to write, write to think* and GEARS guidelines.

"Yes. Ideation can involve the experiencing and processing stages of the learning cycle. In other words, as you immerse yourself in your experience you can imagine the surrounding colors, images, voices, sounds, smells, and textures of being there. And then, we don't know exactly how, but the brain brings together all this multi-sensory information and transforms it into words and actions. Maybe it's like making a smoothie. One second, the separate chunks of ice, pineapple, mango and banana are sitting there in the food processor and the next second, I press the button and they come together in liquid form. Ready to drink. Pretty neat, huh? Can you guess what other stages of the learning cycle might occur while you are ideating?"

"Mmmm. I mean hmmm." Jamie had to stop thinking about the smoothie. She tried to remember what was going on inside of her brain while she generated ideas about a topic and drew her GEARS map. "Maybe a bit of the *concluding* stage, too," she said. "Because after the details are out there, you connect them."

Jamie held up the GEARS Map she had worked on during the week and pointed to the lines between her circles. "See? You connect them. And when you draw these lines to connect your ideas, I guess you end up drawing conclusions, or insights, about your experience."

"Exactly. That's some map, Jamie." Mrs. Flaherty nodded. "I see you liked the circle version. So as our final activity for today, how about walking me through the learning cycle using your map as a guide? For starters, what is the experience that sets your learning cycle in motion?"

"My parents' divorce. See?" Jamie pointed to the circles of supporting background detail near the center of the map. "It was like a storm cloud had hit our family. I was in complete shock. I remember feeling numb."

"Okay. Any examples of the processing of your experience?"

"Well, all these circles of supporting evidence and details. They're all over the place. See? Here's a bunch." Jamie pointed to the section of her map with a cluster of phrases describing her parents after the divorce: Mom took more control; When the toilet broke, she would fix it…; They spent more time with us; Both parents , not just one, would come to school events; etc.

"So how, then, did you get from processing your experience to *generalizing* about your experience?" Mrs. Flaherty asked.

"It just happened," Jamie replied. "I wrote down these details and then I realized each one is a way that my mom or dad changed for the better. I guess the second I connected the details, I was coming up with conclusions about my experience—the generalizing stage of the learning cycle."

"Great!" Mrs. Flaherty exclaimed. "What about the *applying* stage of the learning cycle? How do these changes affect you today?"

Jamie smiled. "I know it sounds like a cliché, but I really *do* realize that every cloud has a silver lining. I am not so down about the divorce anymore. In some ways, our lives are better because of it. I'm not just making this up to have something to write about. The next time I face a crisis, I know from experience that something good could come of it."

Narrate with Insight

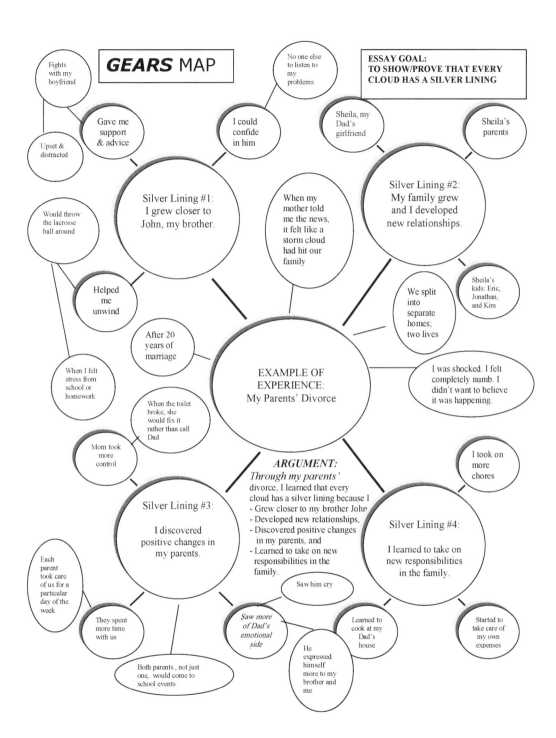

Mrs. Flaherty continued to study the details on Jamie's GEARS Map. "You know, you've come a long way over the last couple of years," she said. "In fact, you've come a long way over the past couple of weeks. I believe that you show such progress precisely because you are skilled at applying what you have learned. When we meet again, we'll talk about the next letter of *think to write*—the *k* for keeping your focus. Now that you have filled out your map and have achieved at least *four* insights from what I see here, your challenge is to chisel this down just to those points that are essential to your argument. This is a lot of material to treat thoroughly in only twenty-five minutes."

As Jamie turned to leave, Mrs. Flaherty gave her one last piece of advice: "Practice walking yourself through the learning cycle this week. When you face a new experience or find yourself thinking about an old one, figure out how you would narrate the *experiencing, processing, concluding* and *applying* stages of the learning cycle in relation to the particular experience."

Jamie knew Mrs. Flaherty was about to give her a handout to accompany the explanation.

Before reaching into her drawer, Mrs. Flaherty challenged her: "Name a food Jamie, that you have always wanted to try but haven't yet had the chance."

"Okay. Goat cheese."

"Great. Imagine that your experience is as simple as trying goat cheese at the dinner table tonight. In the *experiencing* phase; that is, while you are tasting the cheese, you would ask yourself, 'How do I show its taste, smell, texture, etc.—what words do I use to convey the sensory details of my experience?' As for the *processing* phase, you could consider, 'What do I make of all these new sensations—the new taste, the new texture? What is going through my head; what feelings emerge in response to this cheese in my mouth?' During the *generalizing* phase, you would put into words your reaction to the cheese. Your conclusions about it. Your decision—do you like it or not? And to *apply* your experience, address the questions: 'Would I have it again? Would I recommend it to someone else? Would I eat goat cheese on special occasions, or in certain dishes only? What, if anything, have I gained from this experience?' Whether you are trying goat cheese for the first time, stubbing your toe, or arguing with your older brother—you can usually push an experience through the learning cycle and find the words to narrate what is happening at each phase."

As Jamie prepared to leave, Mrs. Flaherty gave her one handout with an outline of the learning cycle, and another with a definition of each phase. "Write as many examples as you can under each heading," she said, "and we'll continue our discussion next week!"

The Learning Cycle
Adapted from David Kolb, 1984

Experiencing

Processing

Concluding/Generalizing

Applying

FOLLOW THE LEARNING CYCLE

Choose an EXPERIENCE as the basis for your argument. *What experience or case from history, literature, technology, politics, current events, or your own life provides the evidence and ideas to support your argument?* The more you connect with your experience or case, the more you will write *with insight.* Relive it, fully immerse yourself in it. Visualize the experience as vividly as possible. In your mind's eye, picture the experience projected onto a movie screen in front of you. *What do you see, hear, taste, touch, feel, or smell in this movie of your experience?*

PROCESS your experience. *What thoughts and ideas pop into your head in relation to the experience? What feelings do you have in association with it?* Think or write quickly and freely. Allow your brain to storm and fill out your GEARS Map.

Draw CONCLUSIONS, gain INSIGHT, learn LESSONS from your experience. Based on the thoughts, ideas, and feelings that you have generated during brainstorming, reflect on the questions: *How, exactly, does this experience or case provide evidence for my argument? How are the ideas I have generated connected to what I am trying to prove: every cloud has a silver lining.* These conclusions will later become the actual reasons you need to support your argument.

APPLY your experience—relate it to the world, to others, and to your future. *How will the insights or lessons you have gained from your experience be used in the future? How will they improve your life or the lives of others? How will they make a difference?*
EXAMPLE: *I hope that my music can affect future generations the way I have been affected by the music of previous generations.*

Chapter Nine

Keep Your Focus

"Catch!"

Jamie crouched down and stuck out her arm to deflect a pink elephant toy that Mrs. Flaherty had hurled her way.

"Catch, not duck!" Mrs. Flaherty laughed. "Speaking of ducks…"

Before Jamie could recover from the first object, a fist-sized blue rubber duck with horns—the kind that floats in bathtubs—flew at her. This time, she reached out and grabbed it.

"Good catch!" Mrs. Flaherty cheered. "I want to try a little experiment to start us off, today, Jamie. We're going to be talking about the k in *think: keeping your focus*. So let's see how many of these objects you can juggle at once."

"But I can't juggle!" Jamie protested, wondering what juggling had to do with writing in the first place.

"That's fine. I can't either. So we'll drop things together. I'll throw you an object; you throw it back to me—and we'll see how many we can juggle back and forth before they start falling." Mrs. Flaherty dug into her *Love My Library* satchel and pulled out a smiling Pillsbury Dough Boy. "Here!" She tossed it to Jamie.

To her surprise, Jamie soon found herself throwing the toys back and forth in synchronized motion with her teacher. The pink elephant, blue duck, and Dough Boy arced over the rows of desks. But the second Mrs. Flaherty threw a fourth object—the bushy-browed Lamb Chops—into to the mix, Jamie faltered. The rubber duck hit the floor with a squeak, and Dough Boy came tumbling after.

"Oops!" Jamie said as Lamb Chops hit her in the mouth.

With a flying leap, Mrs. Flaherty caught the remaining elephant. "So we were doing pretty well with three objects!" she observed. "That last one, though, threw us off."

Juggling Ideas

"Let's try again!" Jamie felt a rush of determination. She still had no clue how throwing silly objects was connected to the *k* in *think*, but she didn't care. This was fun. She swept up the toys and tossed them, one by one, back to Mrs. Flaherty. Quickly, the two resumed their throwing, this time with a menagerie of four instead of three. Until Mrs. Flaherty added a tennis ball. Once again, Jamie fumbled.

"Interesting," Mrs. Flaherty mused. "Seems like three or four are our limit. Any more and we start dropping the ball.

"You mean *I* start dropping the ball," Jamie laughed.

"Juggling is an art," Mrs. Flaherty replied. "My brother, Larry, once tried to explain it to me. He can juggle four objects with ease—quite a feat for someone who was the family klutz. 'The secret to juggling,' Larry said, 'is not in the catching, but in the throwing. Knowing how to throw the object so it comes down to just the right place. If the object is thrown to the right place each time, then you don't even have to think about reaching up to catch it—your hand is already where it needs to be. All you have to do is let the object fall down to your hand.'"

Jamie had never learned to juggle, although once her gym teacher gave everyone in her class three jumbo marshmallows. He had said he wanted them to work on their balance and coordination by juggling the marshmallows. Instead, they ended up having a marshmallow fight. Jamie smiled at the memory of hurtling a marshmallow with all her might at Tom Rivero, who later that day asked her to the Homecoming Dance.

Seeing the Larger Pattern

"It's just like writing," Mrs. Flaherty continued. "To learn a new trick, jugglers have to focus their attention on throwing one object, and the writer has to focus on one idea. But jugglers also have to stay aware of the larger juggling pattern. Did you notice how the toys formed a rainbow overhead when we threw them back and forth to each other?"

Jamie nodded, but her mind had already drifted to the Homecoming Dance. The word *rainbow* instantly reminded her of the mirror disco ball that rotated high above the dance floor. As the ball turned, it created colorful patterns of dancing lights on the gym ceiling. She loved watching them while she danced with Tom.

"Writers, too, have to consider how their ideas fit into an overall story, the larger pattern. Without that sense of the flow of things, writers, like jugglers, can lose control. When we watch a juggler in complete control, our eyes almost pick up the paths of motion, the momentum of the balls in thin air. It's exciting to see and we applaud them as a result. Writers also need to sense the paths their ideas take. They see how their ideas—each one like the elephant, duck, or Dough Boy—flow into a larger pattern of thought.

When we read what they write, we can practically feel the momentum."

"Yeah! I get so caught up in Harry Potter, I can hardly put the book down," Jamie said. "How does J. K. Rowling do it? Keep up the momentum, I mean. Someone told me the idea for Harry Potter just popped into her head out of nowhere while she was on a train or something. Her stories just came to her like magic."

"I don't know, Jamie. I wish we all had some of that magic. But I also believe we make our own magic. Even Ms. Rowling. She, like the rest of us, struggles to keep her ideas going, to keep up the momentum. To make a story flow, she has to first juggle the ideas, launch them in the right direction—you know, like 'throwing' the ideas so they will fall into place. An idea can be colorful and fabulous, but if you don't set it on a path that goes somewhere, how useful can it be?"

Jamie shrugged.

"Ms. Rowling has missed a few book deadlines," Mrs. Flaherty continued. "And she sometimes has to think for a whole week before she works out how something will happen in one of her books. It takes a lot of time and effort for the ideas to fall naturally into place.

"Like the juggler," Mrs. Flaherty continued, "we have to work hard. The more we toss around a few objects, the better our aim gets. That means practice and dropping balls right and left. But when we put our ideas into words, soon they start to flow with direction and purpose. They gain momentum and carry us with their force. They become part of a larger pattern. We learn to *sense* where and how the words will fall.

"Larry once said that the more he practiced and learned to juggle, the less he needed to *see* what he was juggling. As long as he kept his focus, he could sense at what angle and force to throw each ball. Writers, too, learn through practice to keep their focus while they channel their ideas into the words and pattern of a story."

Jamie thought Mrs. Flaherty was getting a little too caught up in her metaphors again. "Maybe if I practiced juggling a little more," she interrupted. But she still didn't see how juggling was connected to writing. How could it help her to *keep her focus*?

"I kept messing up when I had to throw something in one direction and catch something from another direction at the same time. I can only pay attention to so many ideas... I mean objects at once," Jamie felt the urge to defend herself.

"Me too. Let's talk about why. Think about it. When you write a twenty-five minute essay, how many ideas do you realistically have the time to develop?" Mrs. Flaherty asked as she slid into her desk.

"Hmmm. Five?" Jamie guessed, taking a seat up front. She thought of the typical five-paragraph essay with a main idea in each paragraph.

"Isn't it interesting that when we added Lamb Chops and Dough Boy into the back and forth tossing, we could manage four objects at a time? And isn't it interesting that our brains can store on average three to seven chunks of information at a time?"

Maybe five wasn't a bad answer after all, Jamie thought. It fell between three and seven.

"Our brains are like computers," Mrs. Flaherty continued. "Each of us has what we call a *working memory* that, like *RAM*—or the Random Access Memory of our computers—stores data on a temporary basis. When the power is shut off, we lose our data unless we have saved it on the hard drive."

Jamie had learned the hard way what Mrs. Flaherty was talking about. She remembered that time when she was writing a paper on her aunt's old computer and the lights went out. She lost all her work because she had forgotten to press the *save* function as she went along. It was SO annoying.

"RAM can store a certain amount of information only," Mrs. Flaherty said. "Likewise, our working memories can hold onto just so many pieces of information or ideas for a short period of time, let's say half a minute or so, before they fade away or other ideas and information take their place."

Jamie failed to see where Mrs. Flaherty was going with all of this.

"In the same way, we held on to three or four objects before we dropped them," her teacher reminded her. "We had a momentum going. When a fifth object was added, we lost our grip. The shift from catching to throwing and back to catching again was hard to manage with so many objects in the air. The working memory, too, tries to juggle more than one thing at once. It helps us by holding on to an idea while we figure out the words to express it. But we can coordinate only so many thoughts and ideas in working memory before others come along and cause us to shift our focus. Unless we press the *Save* button, we can lose track of the ideas we were thinking about in the first place."

"That sounds about right," Jamie agreed. "Just like when I started messing up. I had one too many toys in the air."

"So, what could you have done about that?" Mrs. Flaherty asked.

"Maybe if I had tossed one of the toys on the desk for the time being or something like that?" Jamie asked, "— Like saving it in the hard drive of my computer.... So I wouldn't have to worry about it. Then I could pay better attention to keeping the other toys in the air."

"Good. So the point is, you should narrow down to three or so main ideas when you write your essay—rather than trying to go with too many ideas at once. Work with only those ideas you can handle at one time. Ideas you can move into an overall pattern—otherwise you might lose your focus."

"So how do I know which objects—or ideas—to keep in the air and which ones to drop?" Jamie asked.

Before Mrs. Flaherty could respond, Jamie was struck by another concern. "And even if I did know which ideas to hold onto, it takes me too long to come up with them. When I did my GEARS Map about my parents' divorce, it took at least half an hour. I wrote down my ideas, but didn't even have time to start writing the essay. What if it was the real test situation?"

"You are still a beginning juggler, Jamie," Mrs. Flaherty said. "My brother dropped a lot of dishes before he could juggle three without a crash.

It takes time to reach that balanced state. Like the juggler, you need to experience over and over again what it feels like to shift back and forth—from one thing to the next, from one idea to another while keeping your focus. As for your question, 'which ideas should I keep and which ones should I drop?' Well ... " Mrs. Flaherty paused to collect her thoughts.

Jamie was getting restless and her mind was starting to wander. "Let's try again," she said, still dissatisfied with her previous performance at catching and throwing. "I bet I could do a better job of juggling if I had another chance. This time, though, let's stand where we can throw the objects to each other easier—closer together and without all the desks blocking us. And let's only use those objects that are easy to work with. Not the floppy and light ones, but those that are more solid—like the elephant. Forget Lamb Chops. She's cute, but too flimsy. "

"Sounds like you're answering your own question about what to keep and what to leave out," Mrs. Flaherty smiled. "And you're figuring out what it takes to keep your focus, too. First, position yourself in a way that you can maintain your balance and concentration. If the desks are in the way, we have a bigger chance of tripping and falling. If we stand closer together, we can more easily throw to each other. Writing also takes physical balance, coordination, and freedom from distractions. In an exam room, I need to sit in the center of my chair, feet firmly on the ground. I need to adjust my arms, neck, head, and back so I can write comfortably and legibly."

"Second," Mrs. Flaherty continued, "you mentioned choosing only those objects that are 'solid' and therefore easier to throw and catch. When we write, we are better off choosing the more substantive ideas from the start—from experiences that are rich and full of detail."

Jamie nodded impatiently. She was ready to roll, objects in hand.

"Okay. Let's try again!" Mrs. Flaherty pushed a desk out of the way and faced Jamie squarely. "Go!"

Once again, the objects whizzed back and forth. Soon, both teacher and student had fixed their eyes on the overhead stream; they no longer had to look at their hands as they threw and caught each object. The objects had a momentum of their own—each a unique toy moving in a pattern, separate and together, both at once.

Jamie felt as if she, herself, was caught up in a magical, effortless current of energy and synchronized motion. She knew that on some level, she was in a state of deep concentration. Her body seemed to know what to do to keep the objects in the air. Her hands seemed to know just how far to throw and just how far to stretch to reach each toy. She also knew on some level that if she thought too much about it, or took her eyes off the overhead stream of objects, she might lose her focus.

"We're good!" Mrs. Flaherty hooted in delight. "How long can we keep this going?"

"Twenty-five minutes?" Jamie guessed.

"I'm afraid I'm going to have to quit before that!" Already, Mrs. Flaherty was slowing her pace. "We still have an essay to talk about before the late bus comes!"

The juggling stopped, and Jamie and Mrs. Flaherty looked at each other, faces beaming. This time nothing had dropped.

"You know, Mrs. Flaherty, You're right. If I pay too much attention to one object and forget the rest, I mess up. I lose my focus. But as long as I keep my eye on the flow of things in the air, I'm fine."

"Hmm. Sounds like you are sensing the connection between juggling and writing. As long as we kept tossing things into that rainbow pattern we created, we could keep three going without dropping them. So to keep your focus while writing, you could limit your ideas to three or so, but you also want to link them to your overall theme or experience—the theme or experience that runs throughout your entire essay."

Jamie's eyes widened. Just when things started to seem clear to her, Mrs. Flaherty would say something to confuse her all over again. What did she mean by linking ideas to an overall theme or experience?

"Remember what we said about pressing the Save button on our computer? We save the information under a specific name. Then, when we need it, all we have to do is go to the drive where we saved it, click on the name of the file and then the name of the document we saved it in.

"Well, our brains work like computers. We save plenty of information in our own "hard drives"—the hard drives of our *memory*, that is. Sometimes, our brains automatically hold onto information without our knowing. And without even trying, we get the information just when we need it. The right file seems to pop up out of nowhere, and that's a lot of fun. The answer comes to us. Like we saw happen the other day, when we watched *Billy Elliot*. The teacher asked Billy to tell her what it felt like to dance, and the answer came to him out of nowhere. He didn't study beforehand. His 'dance file' was so full of experience, he just knew what to say without thinking."

Jamie nodded.

"Other times, however, we have to make a conscious effort to save the information by linking it to something we already know about," Mrs. Flaherty said. "Last weekend, for example, I parked my car in a huge parking garage at the mall. I've learned the hard way I should always write down the letter or number of my parking spot. Well, this time I didn't have a paper or pen handy, so I made a conscious effort to memorize where I was parked. I said to myself, over and over again, *Level 2, Row I; Level 2, Row I…* until finally, it hit me. *2, I, or two eyes!* All I had to do was picture two eyes! Like remembering the name of the document on my computer. Sure enough, when I was done shopping, the image of two eyes flashed in my head, and I found my car quickly."

Jamie's chin rested on the palm of her hand. Her two eyes were focused on the chair in front of her. She was thinking about the Green Day concert she had driven to last weekend with her friends. They were so excited to see the show that no one paid attention to where they had parked the car. It took over an hour to find it…

Mrs. Flaherty's voice cut into her thoughts. "So, after all this talk about how to remember where I parked, how could you *keep your focus* while writing an essay?" she asked.

Jamie shook her head, drawing in her breath. "I'll take a wild guess," she said. "Last week we talked about insight. The lesson we've learned from our experience. You learned to think of two eyes. That's what helped you find your car. I learned to think *every cloud has a silver lining*. That's what helped me get through my parents' divorce.

"So every idea in my essay should be about that lesson. Every idea I choose to remember should support the main thing I've learned from my parent's divorce. I put away all the other ideas—for now. If I can connect my ideas to *every cloud has a silver lining*, then I'll be keeping my focus."

Mrs. Flaherty put her hand over her heart, as if to steady herself. She nodded at Jamie. "Wow," she said, gazing at her student with respect.

"You remembered the learning cycle, Jamie. We don't always start out with such amazing insight. It takes time to get there. Sometimes, we have to sort through our ideas and thoughts and feelings about the experience before the insight comes. How long did it take before we could juggle a few toys without dropping them? Before we learned the secrets to juggling?"

"You know, Mrs. Flaherty. This is deep stuff. Maybe a little too deep for me. I still don't get how to keep my focus. Yeah, I know we talked about shifting back and forth. Shifting from a few ideas to the bigger lesson or overall theme of the essay. But when do I shift? And how do I shift?"

"Every writer has his or her own way," Mrs. Flaherty replied. "We talked about J.K. Rowling. She has a lot of shifting to do. She is famous for weaving intricate webs of ideas into subplots. And then she weaves each subplot into a larger story. And, of course, each story has an important place in the entire series of Potter books. I once heard Ms. Rowling in a radio interview. She explained how she keeps track of what's going on in her books. She creates about twelve 'grid things' for every book, and refers to these grids as a reminder about what has to happen in each chapter to move the plot forward."

"So instead of a GEARS map, she does 'grid things'?" Jamie asked.

"I guess a map and grid serve the same purpose. Instead of little circles, her grids must look like little boxes with notes in them." Mrs. Flaherty replied. "That is what works for her. And as long as we're on the subject of maps and grids, I have a suggestion. Let's see how you actually keep your focus in an essay." Mrs. Flaherty snatched a folder from her file drawer.

Dissecting the Essay

"Here is a file of student essays," she began. "Now pretend we are in science lab, about to dissect something."

Jamie shuddered. Dissect something? Mrs. Flaherty clicked on the ancient overhead projector and placed a transparency in the center of the lighted screen. She played with the focus knob until words emerged out of the fuzzy haze of letters. Jamie recognized the basketball essay from the previous week.

"Now, we are going to start the dissection. Here." Mrs. Flaherty handed Jamie a red pen, glue stick, and double-spaced copy of the same essay that was projected on the screen. "Cut out the central argument—the heart of this essay—by circling it in red."

Jamie circled *losing doesn't break you, it makes you* on her paper while Mrs. Flaherty circled the same words on the transparency.

"Next, we are going to circle all the statements or phrases in this essay that reflect this overall theme, *losing doesn't break you, it makes you.*"

Jamie was delighted that at least a couple of her marks matched the ones on Mrs. Flaherty's transparency. Both of them had circled *our loss did not interrupt the flow of victory;* and, *What we gained from our defeat would make the next victory banner possible.*

"Great!" Mrs. Flaherty said, looking over Jamie's shoulder. "We both picked up on the words this student has chosen to shift back to her overall theme, *losing doesn't break you, it makes you.* Now, like the juggler who keeps the objects moving in an overall pattern, what are the ideas this writer 'throws into' the pattern that drives her argument? Let's underline these ideas."

Two minutes later, Jamie checked to see if her marks matched those of her teacher. They had both underlined: *...I walked off the court towards the locker room, eying the rows upon rows of victory banners that lined the far wall of the gym. I was once struck by how they dated all the way back to 1952. The large gaps between the years were amusing. Sometimes ten, sometimes fifteen—even twenty years would go by before my school won another division title in a particular sport... in spite of those enormous gaps in time between championships, the rows of banners hung in perfect succession. 1952, 1957, 1961, 1969, and so on. Not one line was broken ...Our school's team would regroup and reform until it hit another winning combination—maybe next year, the year after, or even ten years down the road... I realized that like a good book, the part that is left out—what happens " between the lines"—might be the most important chapter of all.*

"See—we both did the same thing. I couldn't help it. I circled everything. I think each sentence feeds into this player's lesson about losing," Mrs. Flaherty realized.

This writer knew how to keep her focus, Jamie agreed. What would she find if she dissected one of her own essays?

"To complete the dissection, I want you to cut out what you have marked and then arrange each piece on a blank GEARS Map," said Mrs. Flaherty, handing Jamie another file. "Notice, Jamie, we are working backwards. Before, we used our GEARS Map to brainstorm the ideas for an essay we hadn't written yet. Now, we are taking a complete essay, dissecting it into ideas, and fitting the ideas back onto the GEARS Map. Notice how each idea is a detail or piece of evidence that supports the overall argument."

Jamie took out of the file a blank circle version of the GEARS Map because, as she explained to her teacher, "it looks like a picture of someone juggling." She thought Ms. Rowling would have liked the more linear, boxy version because it looked like a bunch of grids.

After cutting out the strips of essay, Jamie glued each piece onto a circle. She felt like she was assembling a collage, and each time she pasted down a cluster of words, she could sense the writer's shift from supporting evidence and details to the essay's overall argument; or, from the overall argument to supporting evidence and details. A clear pattern was emerging on the paper.

"This is a good one," Mrs. Flaherty said. As usual, she seemed to read Jamie's thoughts. "The exercise I want you to try this week, Jamie, is the dissection of one of your own essays. By separating and mapping its ideas, you will realize how much you are keeping your focus.

"Double space your essay. Then dissect it by cutting it up just like we did with this basketball one. If any ideas, details, or examples of experience have nothing to do with your main argument, they won't fit on your GEARS map. By mapping your essay AFTER you write it, you can discover where you remained on track and where you derailed from it."

"Okay," Jamie agreed to try.

Getting Ready for the Essay's Content: WRITE to THINK

"We will continue to practice keeping your focus and shifting back and forth from specific supporting details to general ideas as we move on to the actual content of your essay—the WRITE to THINK elements of the writing process. After all, as you *write*, you automatically experience many opportunities to keep your focus. Remember, for example, that the *W* in WRITE stands for *w*riting your introduction, body and conclusion—another type of overall pattern—one that guides the organization of your essay."

Jamie realized that while she remembered the significance of each letter in THINK, she had completely forgotten what W-R-I-T-E represented. No problem. Mrs. Flaherty was just waiting to refresh her memory.

"The *R* stands for *r*eflect on your experience—finding the actual words to best capture your insights, conclusions, and generalizations about your topic. You just said yourself, Jamie, that your insight can be the overall, 'big picture' argument for your essay—what you aim to prove through your experience. What kinds of words, phrases, and sentences, then, shift your own and the reader's focus to the broader meaning of your essay?"

Without waiting for an answer, Mrs. Flaherty continued her explanation of *WRITE*. "*I* stands for *i*llustrate or show the details of that big picture—like finding just the right words to convey the color or the softness or other qualities of the toys that we threw back and forth. Saying 'bushy browed' or 'smiling' or 'menagerie.'"

And *T* stands for the *t*ransitions or words you use to shift back and forth from a specific idea to a general one; or, perhaps, from a body paragraph to a concluding one. After all, you don't want your shifts to be so jerky that they throw you off course, but rather, you want them to be smooth and flowing in one direction. Effective transitional expressions will help you and your reader to stay on track."

Finally, the *E* stands for *e*xpress your ideas clearly. If you can follow some of the basic patterns of language and grammar, you can write in a way that fosters in your readers the energy, momentum, and flow-like state that we experienced while juggling. If you are writing 'in flow,' not only will you forget you are writing, but also, your readers will forget they are reading! Isn't that how the Harry Potter books feel to you, Jamie? You forget you're reading?"

"Yes, but still it's a good thing we have three more months before the next SAT exam," Jamie remarked. She knew that she still had a lot of ground to cover with her teacher and the THINK to WRITE: WRITE to THINK process. "Besides dissecting my essay and seeing how it falls on a GEARS Map, any other worksheets for me to do this week, Mrs. Flaherty?"

"You know what, Jamie? After you have dissected one of your own essays, I think the best thing you can do this week to prepare for the essay exam is to practice juggling."

Was she serious? You never knew with Mrs. Flaherty.

"I mean it! Start out with one object. Then work your way up to two or three. I know that juggling isn't exactly writing, but it sure helps to develop your sense of balance and centeredness, and that shift in focus from one object to the larger pattern of objects. As you juggle, imagine that each object is an idea and that the overall juggling pattern is the central theme or main argument of your essay. All you have to do is to develop a physical sense of how the individual pieces and broader picture relate to each other."

At the supermarket that evening, Jamie threw a bag of jumbo marshmallows into the shopping cart.

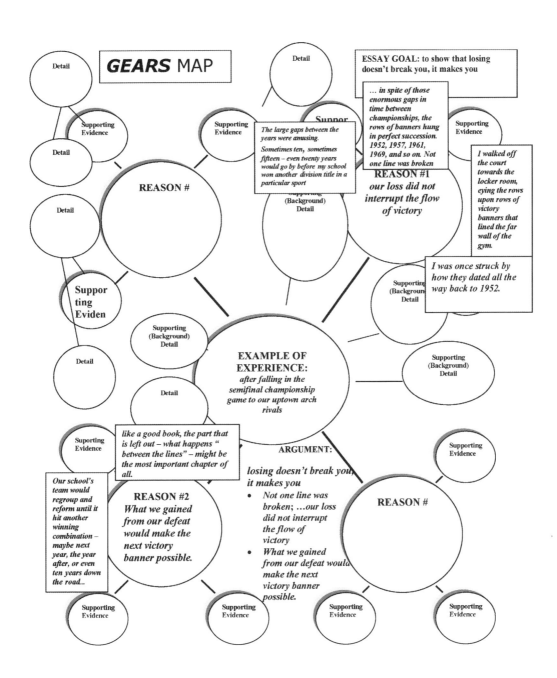

Part 3

W.R.I.T.E. To Think

Chapter Ten
Write Your Introduction, Body, and Conclusion

Jamie felt as if her lungs were going to burst. After a game of flag football and a mad dash to her appointment with Mrs. Flaherty, she stood outside the door struggling to catch her breath. "What next?" she wondered. Would her teacher throw toy ducks and elephants at her the second she walked in?

Jamie entered and looked around. Strange. Mrs. Flaherty was nowhere in sight. But on the board, in big purple letters, were the words: *Riddle of the Day: How are essays like hamburgers?*

"Hmmm," Jamie thought. An image of Mr. Lindstrom, her 6th grade teacher, popped into her head. She recalled his drawing a pretty lame picture of a double cheeseburger on the board, with layers of cheese, ketchup, lettuce, tomatoes, pickles, and onions.

Pointing to his sketch, Mr. Lindstrom said that the parts of an essay were a lot like the parts of a cheeseburger. "The top of the bun is like the introduction," he explained. "It's the first thing we see when we look down at our plate—or paper. It 'covers' the main ingredients of the sandwich, 'revealing' just enough of what lies underneath to make us want to eat—or read on."

The class giggled. Mr. Lindstrom's hamburger looked anything but appetizing.

"Beneath the top, of course, is the juiciest, most interesting part of all—the 'meat' of the hamburger, or the main body of the essay," he said. "All the other ingredients—the lettuce, ketchup, and so on—add color, flavor, and texture to the sandwich. In the same way, writers use 'colorful' details in the body of their essays to bring the main points to life."

Tapping the base of the cheeseburger with his pointer, Mr. Lindstrom continued, "And here we have the bottom of the bun. Along with the top, it helps keep the sandwich together. It's like a stand for the whole cheeseburger, just as the conclusion to an essay is like a final, summarizing stand on the topic."

Jamie was surprised at how much she remembered. *But not my favorite metaphor*, she thought. Her father's latest attempt at meatloaf had been the last straw. She had decided to cut meat out of her diet. Instead, Jamie preferred to compare the essay to a black-bean burrito with salsa, sharp cheddar, and a touch of cilantro.

"Hi, Jamie! Sorry—our teachers' meeting ran late." Mrs. Flaherty's voice broke through Jamie's thoughts. "Did you see my riddle?" she asked.

"Yup," Jamie said.

Mrs. Flaherty's smile turned to a frown. Jamie's silence spoke louder than words. "So you don't like the old hamburger metaphor?"

"I think there's got to be a better way to describe the parts of the essay," Jamie replied. "Maybe we should ask some vegetarians what they think."

Mrs. Flaherty raised her eyebrows. "Well, maybe we can come up with a better image then. We're up to the *w* in our *'think to write, write to think'* strategy. It's time for us to stop focusing on *how* you write, Jamie, and instead, start focusing on *what* you write.

The Content of the Essay

"Up to now, we've been talking about your writing *process*, the steps or actions you take. Now we're going to talk about the actual *content* of your writing. So if a hamburger doesn't do the trick, Jamie—if it doesn't represent the parts of an essay for you, let's figure out what will."

"What does the *w* stand for again?" Jamie asked.

"**W***rite your introduction, body and conclusion.*"

Jamie needed a moment to let the meaning of *w* sink in. "*Write your introduction, body, and conclusion,*" she repeated.

"For many years, Jamie," Mrs. Flaherty explained, "great essay writers have been using this formula to organize their thoughts. That is, they start off with an introduction, usually about one paragraph, and then move into the body of the essay—usually about three paragraphs or so. They finish up with a one-paragraph conclusion. And wallah! They have your typical five-paragraph essay. Doesn't mean *all* essays must follow this formula. But it is the format many writers use starting out. Just like you yourself have been taught since childhood to tell a story in a certain way. Do you remember how you've been told to get started?"

Jamie thought for a moment. "Well, I remember a lot of the stories my parents read me, especially the fairy tales, began with 'Once upon a time.' And they ended with, 'They all lived happily ever after.'

"As I get older, though," she added, "not as many stories seem to end on a happy note." She thought about the *Sold* sign on their front lawn.

"Yup. Real life isn't a fairy tale," Mrs. Flaherty agreed. "In the stories your parents read to you, what happened between 'once upon a time' and 'they all lived happily ever after'?"

The Dynamics of Tension

Jamie paused to think. "Well, the story, itself—I guess. There always seemed to be some kind of conflict, battle, problem, life-and-death situation—some big challenge the main characters faced. I wondered whether they would make it. That's what made the story interesting."

"Hmmm," Mrs. Flaherty nodded. "So a story, then, better have some interesting tension or it might lose its audience."

Jamie smiled. Leave it to Mrs. Flaherty to take what she said and put it into just the right literary terms.

"Essays, too, begin with a sort of 'once upon a time' and end with 'they all lived happily ever after.' Of course, not exactly in these words. All these years, we have been brought up to tell a story with a beginning, middle, and end and to write with the hamburger approach—although the plots in some movies and TV shows I've seen lately seem to jump all over the place. From before the beginning they jump to the end and then to the middle or maybe from after the end to the middle and then back to the beginning."

Jamie was confused. She preferred things to be in simple chronological order.

"Well," Mrs. Flaherty continued, "persuasive essay writers tend to be more traditional than TV shows or movies when it comes to organizing their arguments. They begin at the beginning and end at the ending. And right at the beginning, they introduce some underlying tension, some 'unfinished business,' and develop it throughout the essay. They add just the right amount of detail to build the tension in the body or middle of their essays, and they reach some conclusion or resolution to the tension by the end of their essays. Sort of like 'they all lived happily ever after.'"

"I don't think I introduce any tension into the essay on my parents' divorce," Jamie said. "Even though their divorce was pretty tense, I didn't write about how bad things were. And there was no resolution. My parents are still divorced."

"Keep in mind, Jamie, to show tension, your essay doesn't have to be about a major global crisis or end with a neat, happy resolution. In fact, some of the best stories and essays bring to life everyday forms of tension—the kinds of tension to which we can all relate. For example, the process of achieving insight involves tension. Billy Elliot's tension was his struggle to put into words what dancing feels like. In your essay, Jamie, you are trying to prove that *every cloud has a silver lining*. By making a positive out of a negative, you *are* resolving a tension—a tension between opposites."

Now Jamie was even more confused. She had thought she understood the meaning of tension. Didn't it mean conflict?

As if she could read Jamie's mind, Mrs. Flaherty suggested, "Maybe we should take a look at just what tension *means,* and how it's developed throughout the introduction, body, and conclusion of your essay." She walked over to the bookshelf by her desk.

"We can learn so much from dictionaries, Jamie. So much wisdom can be packed into one neat little word. Dictionaries show us the original roots of words we use every day, and help us understand the essence of their meaning. For example, did you know that the word *essay* means *to try* or *an attempt* to do something? It comes from the old Latin root, *exagiare*, which means *to weigh out* or test. You know, I believe the act of essay writing is, in itself, our *attempt* to explore or weigh out the forces of tension in a situation and see what we can learn from them."

Jamie half rose from her seat, wondering if she should help Mrs. Flaherty move the massive, gilt-edged, foot-thick dictionary off the shelf. But before Jamie could offer a hand, Mrs. Flaherty lifted it with one arm and dropped it with a loud thud on her desk.

While waving away the puff of dust, she began to flip through the pages. Jamie imagined a witch looking through her ancient book of magic spells. And suddenly, like a witch, Mrs. Flaherty cackled. She had found what she was looking for.

"Aha!" Using her finger to trace the fine print, she read, "*Tension: a stretching out…; past participle of the Latin root,* **tendere**, *to stretch out… The physical condition of being stretched or strained.*"

Mrs. Flaherty sounded like she was chanting a spell. "So tension involves a process of stretching or straining!" she exclaimed. "You're right, Jamie, I think we need to come up with something a little more dynamic than a hamburger to describe the parts of an essay. A hamburger doesn't stretch or strain or move in any way until someone picks it up and eats it, of course. Otherwise, it just sits there. An essay has got to be more exciting, to move a little more than a hamburger."

"Well, now that you've defined it, tension makes me think of a spring," Jamie said. "Not the flowers-blooming, birds-singing kind of spring but the kind of spring you find in a mattress. When I jump on my mattress, I'm jumping on a bunch of springs. That's why my mom yells at me. She's afraid I'm going to break them."

"I yell at my kids, too," Mrs. Flaherty admitted. "Jumping causes tension in the coils of the springs. It pushes them together. When you bounce back up, they spring back to their normal shape until your next jump pushes them down together again. I guess I'm afraid *too* much jumping can cause *too* much tension in the springs—and the mattress will lose its shape. Hmmm. I'm not quite sure how we're going to relate *spring* to the introduction, body, or conclusion of an essay. But at least it gets at tension."

Mrs. Flaherty thought for a few moments, and then walked with an exaggerated spring in her step to the blackboard. "I got it, " she said. Clutching a piece of green chalk, she drew a picture of a tightly coiled spring. "Remember the Latin root, *tendere,* meaning *to stretch out*? Well, we find this same root in a lot of words that have to do with the introduction, body, and conclusion of an essay. For example, in the introduction, you write about the in*tention* or purpose of your essay. Your intention, Jamie, is to show in an essay that *every cloud has a silver lining*. Notice that this purpose, itself, presents a form of tension. It poses the question, true or not? People could argue the point. Once you state your purpose, your argument springs into motion."

Mrs. Flaherty redrew the spring, stretching out the coils to form a wavy line. "In the body of the essay," she explained, "you lengthen your argument. Like the coils of this spring. You stretch it out, you expand it by adding the necessary details to support your line of reasoning. For example, you describe how through your parent's divorce, you became closer to your brother. You show us the changes in your relationship—how he became a sounding board when you needed advice about your problems. And because of the divorce, your mother took on roles your father used to play, like fixing the toilet.

"You also tighten your argument," Mrs. Flaherty continued, drawing another picture of a spring with the coils packed so tightly together it looked like a solid bar. "You tighten your argument with the quality of your supporting details—the more solid and convincing your points and the less flimsy your argument—the more likely your readers will agree with you. When you speak from your heart, and use facts to back up your ideas, your reader will have a hard time finding holes in your reasoning.

Mrs. Flaherty drew one more picture of the spring in a relaxed state with a little bit of space between each coil. "Okay. Here we have the spring after the tension is released. It's back to its original form. You've stopped jumping on the mattress, Jamie! In your conclusion, you also release tension by drawing your argument to a close, or by making some final comments on your essay's purpose. For example, you might conclude that every cloud has a silver lining for those who learn to look at the world with optimism and hope. Or you might resolve it takes a lot of time and struggle to produce that silver lining—it doesn't magically appear overnight." Mrs. Flaherty tossed the chalk back into the tray and sat down next to Jamie.

"What do you like better?" the teacher asked. "The hamburger or the spring?"

"The spring is definitely more interesting," Jamie said. "It makes me think of the essay as a moving force. The intro, body, and conclusion don't just sit there like a hamburger—a victim—waiting to be eaten. Instead, they have a say in what will happen to them. They have some momentum going."

"That's right," said Mrs. Flaherty. "The introduction launches the tension, the body tightens and expands it, and the conclusion resolves it. Great! I think we have a new metaphor for the parts of an essay, Jamie!"

Jamie didn't want to ruin her teacher's excitement, but she felt that the spring metaphor wasn't enough. How could it help her to actually *write* the introduction, body, and conclusion?

"I still need to know how to get started, Mrs. Flaherty. Even with the GEARS Map and all the self-talk you suggested, I haven't written the essay yet. Honestly, I'm a little scared..."

Writing the Introduction: Basic Ingredients

"Well," Mrs. Flaherty replied, "the good news is you have already done the thinking required to get your essay off to a strong start. The GEARS Map already contains the tension and other ingredients you need to launch your introduction."

Suddenly, Mrs. Flaherty lowered her voice as if she was about to confide in her pupil a closely guarded secret. "You know, Jamie, before we talk about what these ingredients are, I have a confession to make."

Jamie leaned in a bit closer. She was feeling a little tension in the air, like Mrs. Flaherty was about to reveal a deep dark secret.

"No matter how objective I try to be when I grade an essay, or how many times I tell my students to quit judging a book by its cover—I judge essays by how they start," Mrs. Flaherty sighed. "By the time I finish reading a student's introduction, I can't help it. I've already drawn my conclusion about the entire essay. I can already sense what kind of grade the student will get. Kinda like when you jump on a mattress—you can tell pretty quickly how good the mattress is—how nice and firm—by the first few springs."

Jamie didn't think this confession deserved the look of guilt on Mrs. Flaherty's face. She, herself, could think of far worse revelations. "I guess we all jump to conclusions, sometimes, Mrs. Flaherty," she teased. "I promise your secret is safe with me. What happens though," she asked, "if a student has a great intro but the rest of the essay is lousy? What happens if the student doesn't expand and tighten the argument in the body of the essay or wrap things up in the conclusion?"

"To tell you the truth, Jamie, that doesn't happen too often. If the basic elements of effective introductions are included in the first paragraph, the student has already set the stage to earn a high grade on the essay.

"When I first started teaching," Mrs. Flaherty explained, "I didn't realize the extent to which I was already grading an essay after reading only the first few sentences. But in most cases, my initial perceptions were pretty accurate. If the introduction was good, it helped me to get more out of the rest of the essay—to understand it—and therefore to award a higher grade.

"In fact," Mrs. Flaherty continued, "Last year another English teacher told me a very interesting story. It helped me realize I wasn't alone in grading an essay based on the introduction. She had found a study published over ten years ago in a journal about educational psychology. The authors, from New Zealand, I think, did an experiment to see if the quality of introductions and conclusions actually influenced the grades readers gave to essays."

As Mrs. Flaherty went on about the study, Jamie imagined her teacher revealing a secret far more interesting than her habit of grading an essay before reading the whole thing. What if Mrs. Flaherty was really leading a double life? What if she was an English teacher by day, and at night, she became a writer? What if she was really P. F. Hook, the media-shy author of the best-selling series, *Chronicles of La Sierra High*. In these books, a brilliant sixteen-year-old, Nicky Harris, helps the government crack enemy codes and prevent global crises—problems a lot bigger than someone's parents' splitting up.

P.F. Hook's double life would suit her teacher well, Jamie thought. Mrs. Flaherty seemed to know quite a bit about building tension into stories. Besides, after she went home at night, what happened to her endless ideas? Was her family able to listen and absorb them all? What did she do while the rest of the world slept? Jamie could see her teacher in the wee hours of the morning, eyes glued to the computer screen, fingers flying at the keyboard, while her mind brewed with creative twists and turns to some new plot for Nicky Harris and La Sierra High School.

Jamie struggled to control her imagination and focus on what Mrs. Flaherty was saying.

"The researchers reviewed several guides on writing essays and pulled from them a list of the most frequently mentioned characteristics of effective introductions and conclusions. Then, they gave readers a package of essays to grade. Unbeknownst to these readers, some of the essays had introductions or conclusions that met the criteria for effectiveness and some didn't. In other words, the introductions or conclusions varied in quality from essay to essay based on the extent to which they showed the desired characteristics described in the essay-writing guides."

Jamie felt like her eyes were going to close. She forced herself to sit up straight and take a deep breath.

"Well, in the end, the essays with the most effectively written introductions were awarded the highest grades—even more so than the essays with effectively written conclusions. The authors concluded that the quality of the introduction appeared to have more impact on the final grade for the essay than the quality of the conclusion did."

"I don't get it," Jamie protested, her attention no longer divided. It seemed like Mrs. Flaherty was saying she could raise the grade of her essay by improving the first few sentences. "You mean that the quality of the conclusion doesn't matter?"

"Sure it matters, Jamie. What matters even more is stating very clearly in the introduction what the reader can expect from the essay. Think about it for a second. Imagine that I'm reading the final draft of your essay. The more I understand at the beginning what you're attempting to prove, the more clearly you've stated the intent of your essay, the more I'll get out of the rest of it. If I'm confused about your intent from the start, your conclusion—no matter how great—will be less meaningful to me."

"That makes sense," Jamie nodded. "Sometimes, when I'm peer editing my friends' essays in L.A., I just don't understand what they're trying to say. That feeling, 'I don't get it,' happens to me in the first few sentences. I get impatient and lose interest. But if I do understand what they're getting at, what they're trying to persuade me to think or see, the rest of the essay is so much easier to follow.

"You know, I never really thought about it before. I guess I judge an essay by its introduction, too," Jamie said, and smiled.

"You see!" Mrs. Flaherty was delighted. "I'm not the only one. And you know, Jamie, there's something else I've noticed about writing the introduction, body, and conclusion. Students sometimes go back and polish up their introduction *after* they've written their conclusion. In other words, the conclusion forces them to realize the lessons they've learned from their experience. Remember the learning cycle! Concluding is the phase after experiencing.

"The clearer the lesson is to the writer," Mrs. Flaherty continued, "the more clearly it's worded in the introduction. For example, if I've realized that clouds have silver linings for those who have learned to look at the world with optimism and hope—I can write this point in my introduction and be clearer, from the start, about what I intend to prove in my essay. Seems a bit funny, doesn't it? My best introduction might come to me *after*, not before, I've written my conclusion."

"So what are these criteria, then, for the A+ introduction?" Jamie asked. "I wouldn't mind knowing what makes an effective conclusion, either. Especially if this helps me to write a clearer introduction."

"I have some guidelines that might help you, Jamie. I am sure they're similar to those used in the New Zealand study; plus, I have added a couple more helpful hints from my own readings and experience. You'll see I've included guidelines on the body of the essay, too. We'll spend even more time on this portion of the essay when we explore the rest of the letters in WRITE *to think*."

"So we're done covering the *W in Write?*" she asked as Mrs. Flaherty handed her a booklet.

"Just about. As soon as you master these ingredients of successful introductions, bodies, and conclusions, your essays will improve, and you might even see your grades go up!"

"I could deal with that!" Jamie said.

"Okay then," Mrs. Flaherty said. "I think you should look at the essays you've already written for examples of these ingredients, and if you can't find any, make some up! Or find them in essays by others. They don't have to be SAT essays. Any essay will do. Newspaper or news magazine editorials are good. My hunch is that you'll find these ingredients—maybe in a different order—in those essays that have been awarded the highest grades on the SAT."

Over the next few days, Jamie examined the tables in the booklet Mrs. Flaherty had given her, and found examples for each characteristic from an essay her brother had written on road rage when he was a senior in high school—an essay his teacher had given an *A+*.

Writing the A+ Essay: Master the TEN's

THE INTRODUCTION Setting the Stage for your Essay	
Capture your reader's atTENtion:	
1. Discuss the importance or timeliness of your topic:	
Guiding Questions What is the reason that readers should pay any at*ten*tion to your essay in the first place? What's in it for them? Why should they care?	Example: *As the number of traffic fatalities due to road rage is on the rise, an understanding of how to de-escalate our own or another driver's anger before it gets out of control might be critical to survival on the nation's roadways.*
2. Write an engaging *"clincher"* statement or *"hook:"*	
Guiding Questions How can you grab your reader's at*ten*tion? What compelling idea, image, quotation, question, snatch of humor, metaphor, exclamation, etc., would make your reader curious enough to read on?	Example: *As the car screamed by at over one hundred miles an hour, the unmistakable butt of a shotgun protruded from the driver's window.*
3. Present the underlying TENsion of your essay:	
Guiding Questions What is the *ten*sion you in*ten*d to explore or resolve in your essay? What is the main problem, issue, concern, dilemma, crisis, threat, risk, opportunity, weakness, strength or challenge you plan to address?	Example: *Although road rage has swept the country like a lethal epidemic, most drivers are unaware of the most effective ways to treat it.*

4. Clarify the exTENt of your argument:	
Guiding Questions	Example:
• What is the scope of your topic? • What will be the limits of your argument? • What can you cover realistically within the length and time allotted for your essay?	*An exploration of the three major causes and symptoms of road rage will help drivers to better understand how to manage or even prevent it.*

5. AtTENd to the necessary background information:	
Guiding Questions	Example:
• What does the reader need to know to understand your topic? What background information is vital to your argument? • What unfamiliar terms or phrases need to be defined? • What example/s or experience/s will you present to argue your case?	*Across the nation, the number of traffic fatalities due to incidents of road rage has risen to crisis proportions. In the first five years of this century, hundreds were injured or killed in road-rage related incidents.*

6. Declare your major inTENtion/s:	
Guiding Questions	Example:
• What, exactly, will you attempt to show your reader? • What is the line of argument or reasoning you will use in your essay? • What is your claim, view, or position about the topic? From what stance will you address the underlying tension?	*By understanding the signs and root causes of road rage, we can prevent it from escalating or maybe even from happening in the first place.*

7. ExTENd your introduction to the body of your essay:	
Guiding Questions	Example:
• What final sentence in the intro paragraph would set the stage for a smooth transition to the second paragraph?	*As the number of traffic fatalities due to road rage is on the rise, an understanding of how to de-escalate our own or another driver's anger before it intensifies beyond control might be critical to our survival on the nation's roadways.*

THE ESSAY BODY

1. ExTENd the background information into the body of your essay, if necessary:

Guiding Questions	Example:
• What else does the reader need to know to fully grasp your argument? Can you present these details in the body?	*According to the American Automobile Association, road rage is defined as "uncontrolled anger that results in violence or threatened violence on the road."*

2. Support and mainTAIN your main inTENt in each

Guiding Questions	Examples:
• What is the overall point, main idea, or principal TENet of each paragraph? • Is the main idea/TENet of each paragraph linked to the main inTENt of your essay? • What are the specific details and pieces of evidence to support the main idea/TEnet of each paragraph? What three details or pieces of evidence (reasons, illustrations/sensory descriptions, explanations, facts, concrete observations, comparisons, contrasts, etc.) would provide the strongest support? • What transitional words and expressions will ensure the smooth flow of ideas within and between paragraphs?	*Investigators of road rage claim that when motorists are cut off or tailgated, they often experience a surge of anger.* *Motorists can try a number of relaxation techniques such as deep breathing, counting to ten, or visualizing a tranquil scene to help control their anger when another driver seems to be purposefully cramping their space.* *In addition to these techniques, motorists can imagine that the annoying or aggressive driver has a seriously ill child in the back seat of the car <u>and that this child has to be rushed to the hospital to survive.</u>*

3. AtTENd to alternative points of view:

Guiding Questions	Example:
• What are the counterarguments to your line of reasoning? • What are the advantages and disadvantages to the opposing points of view?	*Some defenders of road rage argue that it is a natural defense mechanism to show aggressive drivers they can't get away with their behavior. Others say that road rage can be prevented by creating more lane lines or shoulders on the highways.*

CONCLUSION
The final opportunity to leave a lasting impression on your reader.

1. Wrap up your *in*TEN*t*: briefly summarize the main ideas of your essay without repeating them word for word:

Guiding Questions	*Example:*
What are the central insights that you explored in your essay? (Keep in mind that a short essay, in particular, does not need a complete restatement of your ideas).	*Road rage, then, begins with the anger that arises when motorists feel slighted by other motorists on the roadway. Those that can learn to manage this anger before it escalates beyond control can keep their road rage to safe levels.*

2. Present your resolution of the TEN*sion* that you posed in the introduction:

Guiding Questions	Example:
• What is the answer to any question/s that you raised at the outset of your essay? • What is the final word in your argument (without introducing a new topic or going off on a tangent)? • What is your final judgment? • What solution do you suggest? • How can you bring your reader full circle? Can you end your essay by returning to an illustration, image, character or other detail you presented in the introduction?	*So when a car screams by at over one hundred miles an hour, the motorist who controls the primal urge to lash back helps fellow motorists counter their instinctive anger and the danger of a negative chain reaction.*

Write Your Introduction, Body, and Conclusion

3. ExTENd your argument to a larger purpose:	
Guiding Questions	Example:
• What are the broader implications of your argument? • What course of action do you propose? • What have you learned by exploring the tension/s in your essay? • What analogies or comparisons can you present to link your argument to a larger purpose? • What warning can you issue to your reader? • What further question can you raise? • What can you predict about the future? • What are the implications or consequences of your argument? • What is your call for action? • What quotation or thought-provoking, unforgettable statement captures the essence of your conclusion? • What image can you paint with words to leave a lasting impression on your reader?	*In today's highly motorized society full of families in the fast lane, the simple effort of learning to count to ten, visualizing a quiet glade in the forest, or leaving the shotgun at home could ultimately save a few hundred lives.*

Chapter Eleven
Reflect on Your Experience: Compelling Telling

Two weeks later, Jamie burst into Mrs. Flaherty's class, breathless again—but this time with excitement. "I went through those handouts you gave me on writing the A+ essay, Mrs. Flaherty," she said, pausing to catch her breath.

"And I used them to write a paper for language arts class. I tried to put in all those things you said to do for successful introductions, bodies, and conclusions. It was hard, but I think it made a big difference in my writing. And you know what? Today Mrs. Craig told me she really liked my paper. I have a feeling she gave me an *A*."

Mrs. Flaherty beamed with pride. "Excellent, Jamie! Are you ready for some more fun?"

Jamie shrank back, waiting for Mrs. Flaherty to throw something at her again.

"I don't mean more juggling," her teacher assured her. "Now that you have in mind a kind of checklist of the main ingredients—the characteristics of the A+ essay—we can improvise like great pastry chefs. They know the basic ingredients to make a cake, but they have fun changing things around. In fact, they might throw away the recipe as long as they remember what people like the most about cakes: an enticing aroma, a moist, light texture, a rich flavor, and so on. In writing an essay, you can also change the order, nature, or quantity of 'ingredients' and end up with some new creation that satisfies your reader."

"I *think* I know what you mean," said Jamie. "We've been taught the formula for the five-paragraph essay ever since Mr. Lindstrom drew that Big Mac on the board in 6th Grade. But I'm not quite sure I'm ready to throw the formula out yet. It makes me feel comfortable. Like I can't go wrong with it."

"You're right, Jamie. When you think about it, you can buy the same Big Mac whether you're visiting McDonald's in Honolulu, Hawaii, or Hillsborough, North Carolina. Isn't that comforting? You can't go wrong no matter where you are! You know you're going to get two all-beef patties, special sauce, lettuce, cheese, pickles, onions on a sesame seed bun!"

"You said that like it was one word!" Jamie exclaimed.

"A little ditty from an old McDonald's commercial, way back in the seventies, I think. Before your time!" Mrs. Flaherty explained. "But that burger's still the same, giving comfort to new generations."

"But didn't we agree last week the five-paragraph essay is a little different from a hamburger?"

"Yes, we did, didn't we? We said that an essay is more dynamic. It has tension. And you can control that tension with the specific ingredients you put into your five paragraphs. They are not dictated to you, the way the formula for a Big Mac is. For example, you can conclude your essay with a line from your favorite song. Or you can come up with an interesting metaphor, or you can make a prediction about the future. As long as you try to resolve the tension you create by connecting your argument to a broader purpose and leaving your reader with something to think about."

"You remind me of my mother," Jamie said. "She goes nuts in the kitchen. She could never work at McDonald's, because the first thing she'd want to do is throw away the formula for a Big Mac. She likes to cut out the unnecessary calories from recipes. She thinks you can always find a healthier substitute for any ingredient as long as you keep in mind 'the effect you want to create.' She says four eggs and a cup of oil will make a carrot cake moist but so will prune whip or applesauce for a lot fewer calories."

"I think your Mom and I would get along pretty well, Jamie. She's right about focusing on the 'effect you want to create.' You can choose from many techniques or ingredients to hook your reader, state your argument, expand on it, tighten it, and end it in a way that makes a lasting impression—the effects you want to achieve in your essay's introduction, body and conclusion. Sounds like you threw some great ingredients together in your essay for Mrs. Craig."

"Hmmm. I never thought of it as cooking," Jamie said.

"Even when we write, we put our chef's hat on," Mrs. Flaherty replied. "This has been a terrific review of *W*, Jamie." The teacher approached the blackboard and wrote in large, green letters: WRITE.

"And today," she smiled, circling the *R* in red, "we're going to talk about one of the most important effects you want to achieve for yourself *and* your reader: the effect of *reflecting on experience*. The very process of writing an essay is, in fact, a process of reflection—the kind of reflection that we talked about in your creation of the GEARS map and more recently, in our meeting on insight, the mark of a high-scoring SAT essay.

"Let's go back to the *N* in *think* for a moment: *Narrate with insight*. What do you remember about the learning cycle?" Mrs. Flaherty asked.

"Well," Jamie paused to think for a moment, "first you experience something, then you process it, then you come up with a conclusion about it and finally you apply what you have learned to your life in some way."

"Excellent." Mrs. Flaherty nodded. "Now here's a question for you: What part of the learning cycle is *reflecting on experience*?"

Jamie felt like she was on a quiz show. "Well," she reasoned aloud, "you said in the *experiencing* phase, I take the experience in through my senses— I see, hear, taste, touch, and smell what is going on around me. As I begin to *process* the experience, I start to sort through my thoughts and feelings about it."

Mrs. Flaherty kept nodding.

"I guess *processing*, then, is *reflecting on experience* because I am thinking back on something... But wait. Isn't the *concluding* phase of the cycle also *reflecting on experience* because I come up with lessons or insights about it? Like the lesson I learned from my parent's divorce: *every cloud has a silver lining*. Or Billy Elliot's insight that dancing is like flying."

"You are absolutely right. And what about the *applying* phase of the learning cycle?" Mrs. Flaherty encouraged Jamie to continue.

"Well, maybe *applying* has to do with *reflecting on experience*, too. After all, the lessons that I apply come from my reflections," Jamie guessed.

"Nice, Jamie." Mrs. Flaherty seemed satisfied with Jamie's response.

"So that's it?" asked Jamie. *Reflecting on experience* is about the processing, concluding, or applying phase of the learning cycle? I thought you said we were going to talk about the *content* of the essay."

"We had to review the learning cycle before getting to the content of your reflections. You're right, Jamie. The letters of *THINK* stand for ideas about the *processes* of essay writing; the letters of *WRITE* represent the actual *content*.

"So what does *reflecting on your experience* look like? What are words you can use to best tell us about your reflections? That's what we are going to talk about today. Time for some more how-to's."

Jamie pulled out her notebook and poised her pen to write.

"Okay." Mrs. Flaherty said as she pulled a file from her desk drawer without looking. "I'm going to read you some examples of *reflecting on experience* from student essays. Listen carefully and tell me what they have in common."

Jamie leaned forward.

I realized Mr. Foster was the best teacher I had ever had.
Swimming in Eel Lake can be a frightening experience.
My little brother is annoying.
My next-door neighbor is a nuisance.
The soccer coach knew how to inspire her team.
Harrison Ford is a hero in movies and in real life.
Aunt Tilda is deathly afraid of four-legged creatures.
George Washington was tall in more ways than one.
Parents have no right to track their children with electronic devices.
Sometimes we should leap before we look.

Mrs. Flaherty stopped reading and looked at Jamie. "Notice anything?" she asked.

Jamie shrugged. Nothing came to mind.

"You don't observe anything that these sentences have in common?" Mrs. Flaherty seemed shocked.

"Well," Jamie hated to disappoint her teacher. "I suppose I have to hear a little more to figure out what is going on with them. I'd love to hear the rest of the essay on tracking children with electronic devices."

Mrs. Flaherty tilted her head in thought. "Hmmm. Maybe that's the point, Jamie. A reflection, alone, isn't enough. You want more."

Jamie didn't know exactly what she had said that her teacher approved of.

"Maybe this will help me to make my point," Mrs. Flaherty continued. "Let me read you another set of sentences, and tell me the difference between these sentences and the previous ones."

Jamie listened carefully.

As I treaded the murky water, an icy hand suddenly grasped my ankle.

When my friends come to visit, my little brother acts as if he is a wriggly puppy, jumping on everyone's lap for attention.

When I come home, day or night, my neighbor is always sweeping her porch and watching me out of the sides of her dark, beady eyes.

After every victory, she would order us greasy pizzas from Romero's.

They marched with white coats and shiny black boots, heels clicking in unison.

The blood dripped, then flowed from the wounds...

"Okay. This time, it is much easier to guess what they have in common," Jamie cut in. "Now I see what you are talking about."

"What?" Mrs. Flaherty asked.

"I mean I can actually *see* what you are talking about." Jamie repeated. "I can picture or even feel what each sentence is describing: *The murky water, the icy hand. The wriggly puppy. The sides of her dark, beady eyes. The greasy pizza. The white coats, shiny black boots, clicking heels.* These sentences have plenty of specific details. The sentences you read before were harder for me to picture. The words and ideas were too general.

"That's precisely my point, Jamie. Reflections on experience are expressed as generalizations, beliefs, opinions—the thoughts we arrive at in the concluding phase of the learning cycle. But you noticed, Jamie, we can't *see* our reflections. They are abstract thoughts; so, unless we use concrete illustrations or descriptions to bring them to life, the reader won't actually be able to see our experience. Reflecting on experience is what we *tell*, and illustrating that experience, or painting a picture with colorful words, is what we *show*. If we want our essays to be interesting, we need to find the words to both tell the big picture, the abstraction, and also show the details of our experience.

Jamie's mind wandered back to her show-and-tell days in the first grade. Every week, her teacher had made each student pick a mystery item for show and tell. The catch was, they weren't allowed to show or name the item. They had to tell the class about it or describe it until someone guessed what it was. Sometimes, the guessing was easy: *It's red. It has wheels and goes fast. It has a loud siren. It puts out fires...* was a cinch compared to *I like it a lot. It is very, very big and special. I got it from the store.*" That one was not only hard to guess, but annoying.

"Next week," Mrs. Flaherty's voice broke into Jamie's thoughts, "we'll talk more about the techniques you can use to *illustrate* or show your experience. Today, however, I want you to leave here knowing what effective *telling* is all about. Once you have mastered the arts of telling and showing, and moving back and forth between these two techniques when you write your essay—you will be even further along the road to achieving top grades at writing."

"Oh! I almost forgot!" Jamie said. Mrs. Flaherty's discussion of telling and showing reminded her about the article on SAT essays she had cut out from the local newspaper that week. She fumbled in her bag for the clipping.

"Here." Jamie handed Mrs. Flaherty a long strip of newsprint. "Read the last paragraph."

Mrs. Flaherty reported in a newscaster voice: " 'My main advice,' one SAT essay rater suggested, 'is for students to be more specific in their writing. I read countless essays that contain one sweeping general statement after another. These essays need supportive details to earn a higher score.' "

"That's exactly what we are talking about!" Jamie said. "Is there such a thing as too much telling?"

"You're getting to the heart of the matter, Jamie! Too much telling and not enough showing is the downfall of many student essays. For example, as you yourself realized, the first sentences I read to you were general ones. They left you hanging, waiting for more details so you could complete the picture in your mind. Now let me read something a little different. This is not a set of unrelated general statements; these are related. A whole paragraph. This is the second paragraph from the body of a student essay on *My Favorite Hero*. Tell me what you think:

"I am very close to my father. He has taught me a lot about independence and growing up. He is the major hero in my life and always supports me in whatever I want to do. I would not be the person I am today if it weren't for my Dad."

"I'm left hanging again," Jamie admitted. "I have the same sense I did before when you read the general sentences—I can't see what the person is thinking and feeling—how they see things. I need more."

After critiquing her peer, Jamie added sheepishly, "I bet my writing is like that, too, though."

"Maybe. This student is writing from the concluding phase of the learning cycle. She is giving us a whole bunch of general conclusions about her relationship with her father—a great way to tell us the big picture. But she doesn't show us how she arrived at these conclusions or how she applies them to her life. As a result, the reader can only scratch the surface of what makes Dad her favorite hero. I'm sure the writer has kept the details of the relationship inside of her, without realizing that the picture she has presented is so vague. Good *telling*, but not enough showing to absorb the reader. What could the writer do to make it better?" Mrs. Flaherty asked.

Jamie couldn't believe how easy it was for her to criticize an essay—as long as it wasn't her own: "For starters, she could show us more about what the father actually did to be close to his daughter. Maybe, for example, he sat down with her and read three bedtime stories a night until she was seven years old. And how, exactly, did he teach her independence and show his support? Did he give her the keys to his new car when she got her learner's permit?"

"Excellent. You are suggesting some techniques of showing—dialogue and action—that would help us *see* what is unique about this father-daughter relationship. Instead, the student stops after giving us some general statements. We can only guess what 'close' means to her.

"And my experience of a 'close' relationship," Mrs. Flaherty added, "might be very different from her experience or even your experience of a close relationship. So again, let's keep in mind that effective telling, such as declaring the main idea or topic sentence of a paragraph, needs to be accompanied by good showing if we want to engage our readers' interest and enable them to see from our perspective."

"Why bother with telling in the first place if it is downright boring?" Jamie asked.

"Well, you're right. An essay that is *too* general with *too* much telling and not enough showing is boring. But without any telling at all, we might have a hard time grasping the central point or purpose of the argument. After all, the overall intent of the essay, the main idea of each paragraph, and the wrap-up of ideas in the conclusion are usually told to us. They help us to keep track of the bigger picture—the writer's overall argument. Keep in mind, persuasive essays, in particular, require a balance of showing and telling. On the other hand, if I were writing an adventure story or personal narrative, I might rely a little bit more on showing to engage my reader."

"All right, then," Jamie conceded. "If I have to *tell* in my SAT essay, how can I *tell* in a way that is as engaging as showing?"

Mrs. Flaherty smiled. "Well. Let's take a look at the different techniques of telling and you can judge for yourself whether they are engaging or not. But first, I think we need to clarify what qualifies a statement as *telling*."

Jamie could have guessed. Time for the trusty dusty dictionary. Within seconds, Mrs. Flaherty was quoting from her super-sized Merriam-Webster:

" 'Tell —to *narrate, make known, divulge, reveal, inform, order, direct, know or recognize... from the old German word for to count and the old English word for tale.*' "

Mrs. Flaherty closed the book with a loud *klumpf* and eyed Jamie. "Makes sense. Since we are talking about *reflecting on experience*, *telling* is our attempt to share with the reader what we have found out as a result of reflecting. We can tell what we have learned in a number of different ways."

Mrs. Flaherty already had a pile of handouts waiting for Jamie on her desk. She handed one to Jamie. "Remember, when we tell, we are expressing our thoughts or realizations from the *processing* and *concluding* phases of the learning cycle. To put it simply, in telling, we state what we know or believe to be true based on our experience. Let's look at some examples."

Jamie read:

A's: Assertions, Assumptions, Analyses

<u>Assertions</u> – **Positive statements or declarations** about experience that are made with confidence and force.

- *SAT scores shouldn't be the only factor in evaluating a candidate for college admission.*

- *This financial aid information must be made available to all those in need.*

- *Even though she initiated the divorce, she has a right to a portion of the property.*

<u>Assumptions</u> – Statements, beliefs, facts, or notions that are taken for granted.

- *His war injury prevents him from engaging in rigorous physical activity.*

- *Our parents will always be there to love and help us.*

- *In this organization, who you know is more important than what you know.*

<u>Analyses</u> – Observations, remarks, statements of fact or findings based on patiently looking at, paying attention to, carefully studying, taking apart, putting together, considering, watching or noticing something.

- *Couples with lasting marriages attribute their success to their skills of active listening, patience and respect.*

- *I've learned through life experience that honesty is indeed the best policy.*

- *He was fired from his full-time job at the restaurant because of his chronic lateness and absenteeism.*

- *The inmates soon discovered that all of their escape routes led to shark-infested waters.*

- *The test was difficult because of the large number of questions and short amount of time we had to answer them.*

B: Beliefs

<u>Beliefs</u> – Firmly held opinions, ideas, or feelings about people, situations, or events.

• *No one is ever one hundred percent right or one hundred percent wrong.*

• *Employees should be promoted on the basis of merit, not seniority.*

• *Our state government should lower the drinking age to eighteen.*

C's: Conclusions, Concepts, Conceptualizations

<u>Conclusions</u> – Opinions, comments, positions, viewpoints, judgments, decisions, or propositions achieved after thought, consideration, or logical reasoning.

• *I've decided that I like your idea about a senior class holiday.*

• *This movie will definitely be a blockbuster.*

• *Because of the total lack of publicity, the dance was cancelled.*

• *In view of the latest statistics, one would think that marriages are meant to be broken.*

<u>Concepts</u> – General ideas, abstractions, or inferences formed on the basis of observing specific events.

• *Wealth can destroy.*

• *Power and responsibility go hand in hand.*

• *Freedom is a state of mind.*

<u>Conceptualizations</u> – Expressions of a particular way of perceiving something, or of an awareness or knowledge of something.

• *Spare the rod and spoil the child.*

• *The more the merrier.*

• *This mural makes a brutal statement about life in the 17th century.*

D: Directives

<u>Directives</u> — Instructions, pronouncements, or orders that are issued with authority and aimed toward a specific goal or action.

- *We must pay special heed to the growing restraints on student freedoms in our school district.*
- *Fight or perish!*
- *Unless he starts getting some regular exercise, his heart will grow weaker.*

E: Explanations

<u>Explanations</u> — Statements, clarifications, thoughts, rationalizations, and declarations that make something more understandable.

- *The show was delayed because the star actress passed out cold twenty minutes before the opening curtain.*
- *He didn't show up to baseball practice because his teacher gave him after-school detention.*
- *The ski resort is suffering because of the warm winter.*

F: Facts

<u>Facts</u> — Concepts, statements, or assertions of information that are indisputably true.

- *Martin Luther King died on April 4, 1968.*
- *Water consists of two parts hydrogen and one part oxygen.*
- *Mother's Day falls on the second Sunday in May.*

G: Generalizations

<u>Generalizations</u> — Statements, ideas, laws, propositions, reasoning, or principles that have been deduced from particular facts or details and have general application.

- *People prefer to drink red wine with an Italian dish.*
- *The children in the Meyer family don't know how to behave.*
- *In this particular culture, patting a child on the head is considered an insult.*

H: Hypotheses/Theories

<u>Hypotheses/Theories</u> — Concepts, proposals, opinions, assumptions, interpretations, or suppositions, based on incomplete evidence, but if proven, would explain certain observations, facts, or phenomena.

- *His twice-a-day French fry habit may be the cause of that acne.*
- *If the speed of metamorphosis is related to temperature, then exposing cocoons to higher temperatures will cause the butterfly to emerge sooner.*
- *Perhaps the reason for her falling asleep in class is the addition of a new baby brother to her family.*
- *A cosmic explosion created our universe.*
- *Gravity prevents us from floating in space.*

I: Inferences

<u>Inferences</u> — Conclusions based on previously drawn conclusions or circumstantial evidence rather than direct observation.

- *The earth is flat.*
- *Women aren't fit for the world of boxing.*
- *He should go to jail for his pranks.*

J: Judgments

<u>Judgments</u> — Conclusions, opinions, decisions, evaluations or assessments about people, situations or events.

- *Video games reinforce aggressive tendencies in children.*
- *Video games enable children to learn new patterns of thinking.*
- *The children need more exercise.*

Jamie looked up at Mrs. Flaherty. "Thank goodness you stopped at *J!* I'm not sure my brain can take in all these techniques!"

"I don't expect you to memorize them, Jamie. Just *familiarize* yourself with them. Go back and look them over several times before you take the SAT or write a paper."

"And so many of these ways of telling are alike," Jamie observed. " Is a conclusion all that different from a judgment? Or can an assumption also be a belief?"

"Certainly. Many of these ABC's of compelling telling overlap. Or one way of telling encompasses the other. Most of them though, have something in common. Can you guess what that is?"

Jamie looked over her handouts for another moment. "I'm not sure, but it looks like you want me to think like a detective or lawyer to write a persuasive essay."

"Good point, Jamie. Almost all of these *ABC's*, except for *facts*, require further evidence. Otherwise, unless they are statements of common knowledge, the reader has no proof they are true."

"Yeah—how do I really know marriages last if the husband and wife respect each other?" Jamie asked, referring to the analysis of couples staying together. "I may have a different experience. All the respect in the world didn't help *my* parents to stay together."

"You're right, Jamie," Mrs. Flaherty said softly. "All it takes is one exception to refute any of these arguments. That's what each of these examples has in common. After all, most of these ways of telling are, in fact, disputable. This brings us back to our original point. The need to support your telling by showing. If a student burst in here, for example, to *tell on* another classmate, should I take her story as the truth?"

"If she were telling on me, I'd be mad!" Jamie replied. "I would hope that, as the teacher, you wouldn't jump to conclusions about me. You'd give me a chance to defend myself. And you'd ask the student to prove it."

Mrs. Flaherty nodded. "What if that student ran in here screaming, *Get out, the roof is about to cave in!*"

"I'd look up! Jamie said automatically.

"So before you run for your life, you would first want to *see* that the roof is about to cave in?"

"I guess, " said Jamie. "It doesn't take much to look up. Even if I didn't know the student very well, I'd probably believe her. Especially if I could see the terror in her eyes. That would make me terrified, too."

"I think the same thing applies to essays," Mrs. Flaherty mused. "I mean, your readers will believe you if you are sincere. If you tell and show what you honestly think and feel. The art of persuasion, then, is to use a combination of telling in ways that reveal the big picture, so the reader has an eye on the point you're making, and showing in ways that immerse the reader in the real-life details of the experience. So you're juggling several ingredients at once."

Jamie glanced at her watch and gasped. "The bus!"

"You don't have to *tell* me it's time to go," Mrs. Flaherty laughed. "I can see it in your face! Practice your telling this week, Jamie. Come up with your own example for each of the ABC's of compelling telling. And I'll see you after the break!"

"Have a great Thanksgiving, Mrs. Flaherty!" Jamie expected she would have a lot of compelling family TENsion to tell about over the next few days.

Chapter Twelve
Illustrate Your Experience: Showing

"I think I figured it out, Mrs. Flaherty." Jamie announced after Thanksgiving break.

"Oh?" Mrs. Flaherty raised her eyebrows.

"If I'm ever going to do any *compelling telling*, I have to *like* what I'm writing about. I learned that the hard way. Have you ever read anything by Edwin Boring?"

Mrs. Flaherty shook her head.

"Well, *Boring* is boring. Mr. Dillon, in history, asked us to write a paper on something to do with scientific revolutions, and when I *googled* the topic, I came up with a link to Edwin Boring and something called *Zeitgeist*. I had no idea what Zeitgeist meant, but when Mr. Dillon wanted to know what we had chosen to write about, I tried to sound smart. I said Boring and *Zeitgeist*. I thought Mr. Dillon would laugh along with everyone else, but instead, he was so impressed he promised me extra credit! He said *Zeitgeist* was an SAT vocabulary word. I should've kept my mouth shut." Jamie rolled her eyes.

"The next thing I know, I'm trying to read this book by Boring called *The History of Experimental Psychology*. It's as thick as your dictionary, Mrs. Flaherty. And the whole book is all telling, no showing. I was so confused and frustrated. I just didn't understand it. I had to keep rereading the first chapter to get the meaning of *Zeitgeist*.

"Finally, I got it. I realized that *Zeitgeist*, German for *spirit of the times*, is what makes ideas like Ipod or Facebook so popular. The kids my age are so used to instant connections. In seconds, we can be listening to our favorite song or sending a message to our best friend. No matter where we are or what we're doing—we don't have to wait. My *parents* didn't have that when they were growing up. Did you, Mrs. Flaherty?"

"Nope. We had to wait for snail mail, play music on record players, and if we wanted to make a phone call, we had to find a telephone booth and beg for quarters.

Jamie didn't know how Mrs. Flaherty survived. "I got so excited by my..., well, by my *insights*—you know, the third phase of the learning cycle—that I wrote all night long. Ideas kept popping into my head. I even put your handouts on the ingredients for writing an A+ essay in front of me, and used all of them." Jamie was glowing.

"And was your telling compelling?" Mrs. Flaherty asked with a smile.

"Well, not at first. But as soon as I started to like my topic, it got better." Jamie explained. "Once I could relate *Zeitgeist* to something I knew about—something in real life, the more I got into my writing. And the more I kept writing, the more I understood what *zeitgeist* means. All sorts of examples and ideas came to me. Maybe that's it. I had to really make sense out of *Zeitgeist* before I could show or tell about it. As soon as I could experience it in my mind, as soon as I could relate it to my own experience, the words to describe it came easily."

"Can you tell me, in a nutshell, the sense you made out of an abstract concept such as Zeitgeist? I'm a little rusty myself. Good thing I don't have to take the SAT! Now that you've refreshed my memory, Jamie, I realize I haven't used that vocabulary word since writing term papers in college," Mrs. Flaherty admitted.

"Besides," she added, before Jamie had a chance to answer her question, "I thought that today, trying to label the 'spirit of the age' is next to impossible. We live in an uncertain, chaotic, multicultural world—one that is too complex to capture in a single *Zeitgeist*."

In the next instant, Mrs. Flaherty sprang from her chair, eyes burning as if a light had flashed inside her head. "Jamie, you've given me an idea!" The thrill in her voice rang like a preacher's *Hallelujah* as she ran to grab a piece of green chalk.

"You know that today we are going to talk about the *I* in WRITE, right? '*Illustrate*, or *show* your experience.'" She dashed the sentence on the blackboard.

Jamie nodded.

Painting a Picture with Words

"Unlike *telling*, or reflecting on experience, *showing* is about painting a picture of that experience with words. Instead of just writing *about* the experience, you also recreate it for the reader to see, hear, taste, touch, smell, or feel. Remember, Jamie? We discussed combining your telling with showing so your reader can actually *see* the details of your argument and get a better sense of how you arrived at your conclusions."

"Yep." Jamie nodded. After a whole night of writing a paper on *zeitgeist*, she had experienced firsthand how hard it was to balance telling and showing. At the same time, the more she went to the trouble of showing what she was telling, the more she *liked* what she was writing.

"So instead of just *telling* us, 'He had a very bad cough at night,' and leaving it at that," Mrs. Flaherty continued, "we are more likely to be convinced the cough is bad if you *show* us—'the hacking jolted me from my sleep.'

"How about a quick review—I give you five more examples of telling and showing—and you tell me which is which!" Mrs. Flaherty suggested. "For each example, I'll say it in a way that is telling and in a way that is showing. Just mark down which part—the first or the second part of the example—is showing."

"Okay," Jamie said, readying her pad and pencil while Mrs. Flaherty read from a paper at her desk:

"1) The muscles tightened in my neck. **Or**, 2) I was angry.

"1) *John, stop lying to me!* I scream at him inside my head. **Or**, 2) I wish John would be more truthful. It makes me angry when he lies like this.

"1) 'I'll make it home for Christmas this year,' John promises me. *I know he will not be back at Christmastime, New Year's, Easter, or ever. I won't see him for years. We both know it.* 'Okay,' I murmur softly, choking back the tears. 'See you at Christmas.' **Or**, 2) John always says he'll come home soon, even though we both know that I probably won't see him again for a long time. I pretend to believe him when he says that he'll be back. I don't let him see I am crying.

"1) I crashed and stumbled through the bushes, wrenching arms and legs free from the sharp, piercing thorns. The more I fought, the more the thicket ensnared me. The blood dripped, then flowed from my wounds. Or, 2) I tried to run through the bushes. My arms and legs got caught in the thorns. The more I tried to break free, the more entangled I became. My scratches started to bleed profusely.

"1) The sky covers the lake like a thick black blanket. The boat blends into the darkness. **Or**, 2) It is so dark that you can't see the boat on the lake."

By the end of Mrs. Flaherty's examples, Jamie was laughing. If this was a pop quiz, she had aced it. The first part of each example had to be showing, the second part had to be telling.

"Is it so obvious?" Mrs. Flaherty smiled.

"I can tell which one is *showing* by the expression in your voice alone," Jamie replied. "You sounded like a great actress when you gave the first part of the example, and then you sounded downright boring—your voice had no expression—when you gave the second part of the example."

"Oh?" Mrs. Flaherty feigned surprise. "I guess I couldn't help it. Telling *feels* more boring. If all I did was tell, I bet I'd put my readers to sleep. At the same time, though, I could go to the other extreme. *Too* much showing is like overacting. It will flood my readers' senses. And my essay will be too wordy. So I must show *sparingly* and *selectively*. You know how we say, 'A picture is worth a thousand words?'"

Jamie nodded.

"Well, one powerful, precise word like *hacking*, or a phrase like *thick black blanket* can be enough to paint that thousand-word picture."

Jamie wondered if she would ever learn how to show *sparingly* and *selectively*. It sounded like an art—something professional writers knew how to do. Not high school amateurs.

"I *was* going to show you two things today, Jamie," Mrs. Flaherty's voice cut into her thoughts. "First, a way to look at the process of shifting back and forth from telling to showing; and second, the actual ways to show and engage your reader. But then with all your talk about *zeitgeist,* you inspired me to *rewrite* today's lesson!"

As usual, Jamie was clueless. What did *zeitgeist* have to do with the art of showing and telling?

"For years, Jamie, to explain the thought processes behind showing and telling, I have been showing my students how we climb up and down what is called a *Ladder of Abstraction*. I learned about the ladder from Dr. Hayakawa, a teacher at Harvard University, who wrote about it in his book, *Language in Thought and Action*."

Jamie had a feeling that they were about to discuss another book as thick as Boring's *The History of Experimental Psychology*.

"The original version of this book was written decades before you were born, Jamie," Mrs. Flaherty seemed to read Jamie's thoughts. "But the *Ladder of Abstraction* makes sense even today. It's a way of looking at the words we use to convey our experience, and it helps us to see how the degree of showing and telling in our writing or even in our conversations with each other can change the very meaning of what we are saying."

Jamie tilted her head as Mrs. Flaherty drew what looked like a white ladder on the board, angled slightly, with a few clumps of yellow grass at the bottom and white clouds at the top.

"Notice that this ladder has to be planted on firm ground to remain steady," Mrs. Flaherty explained. "The school around us stands on a strong foundation of concrete to keep from falling. When we describe something, we sometimes choose concrete words—ones that immediately grab our senses—to plant a solid picture of meaning in the mind. For example, I could say, *the grass grew parched and brittle as it baked in the scorching sun*."

While Mrs. Flaherty wrote the words *parched, brittle grass* and *scorching sun* at the bottom rung of the ladder, Jamie imagined grass so dry it crunched under bare feet.

Mrs. Flaherty continued to write descriptions at each step of the ladder. "As I climb up to the next rung, I could explain that for twenty-one days straight, let's say, from August 20th through September 10th of last year, temperatures had exceeded 98 degrees Fahrenheit and not a drop of rain had fallen. At an even higher rung, I could call this period the great dry spell of the decade. Finally, at the top rung of the ladder, the one that is dotted by my clouds here, I could mention we were in the midst of a serious drought. Notice that the term *drought* is far more abstract and 'nebulous' than the words *parched, brittle, and scorching*."

Nebulous. Somewhere, from the recesses of Jamie's brain, the SAT vocabulary section immediately ground into motion: *Cloudy, hazy, vague, ill-*

defined ..., an electronic voice droned from within. Jamie was startled at how much her mind could automatically recall the vocabulary words she had studied.

"Do you notice what happens as you climb from the bottom to the top rung of the ladder?" Mrs. Flaherty asked.

"You start out with concrete, sensory details to describe the dry grass, and end up with a more general statement about the drought," Jamie observed.

"That's the idea!" Mrs. Flaherty nodded. "As we climb the ladder, we are moving from specific to general, or from concrete *showing* words to more abstract *telling* ones. Now what if I started off at the top of the ladder and told you we had a drought without offering any further information?"

"Well, then it could be any drought," Jamie said. I'd probably wonder when did it happen and how bad was it and did it affect the farmers and water supply and things like that."

"So as I provide you with more specific information about the drought, I move back down the ladder. With each rung I climb down, I give you a progressively more detailed description of what the drought looked like to the point of your imagining parched, brittle grass in a specific place and at a specific time.

"Let's try a couple more examples, Jamie. Remember, I said you gave me the idea to rewrite this lesson. Because after all, it's as old as my dictionary over there. I think the Ladder of Abstraction could be updated in tune with today's Zeitgeist—with Ipod's and youTube. But first, before we write the new lesson, we have to master the old one!"

Mrs. Flaherty sketched another ladder on the board; this time, with a spotted cow eating green grass at the bottom and a money sign at the top.

"In the book I mentioned, Dr. Hayakawa uses the famous example of Bessie the Cow. He places Bessie, a real live cud-chewing organism with all her bones, intestines, blood, milk glands, *moos,* and typical cow behaviors at the bottom of the ladder. At the rung above, he inserts the word *cow*—the category of animals to which Bessie belongs. One rung up from cow, he uses the term *livestock* to include not only the cows, but also, Rover the dog, Wilbur the pig, Misty the horse, and any other animals of the farm.

"As he climbs up each successive rung of the ladder, he selects the words *farm assets*, *assets*, and finally—*wealth*, to show progressively broader levels of generality. By the time he reaches the top of the ladder, the real live Bessie is no longer in the picture. We could milk Bessie when she was on her own, a real live cow, but not when she is subsumed under the abstract concept of *wealth.*"

Slowly, the idea of moving from specific up to general and back down to specific again was becoming clearer. Yet Jamie hoped for another example. And she hoped Mrs. Flaherty would get back to her point about showing *sparingly* and *selectively.* She didn't have to wait long. Her teacher was already sketching another ladder on the board.

"We frequently tend to express ourselves in general terms, Jamie," Mrs.

Flaherty said. "How often do you tell your friends you had a good time at the party, or you really liked the movie a lot and you leave it at that without going into any details about your experience?"

Before Jamie could answer, Mrs. Flaherty continued, "I know I'm the biggest culprit when it comes to being overly general. I might say, 'good job' to a student or write 'excellent' on a paper and neglect to describe what, specifically, I liked about it."

"But wouldn't it be hard to *always* be so specific? Wouldn't it tire you out to work that hard to express exactly what you mean?" Jamie asked.

"Yes, it would. Too much specificity is overwhelming—I'd have to spend the rest of my life writing comments on student papers. And I'm not sure my students would really read them if they were so detailed. Sometimes, Jamie, we have to take mental shortcuts and rely on *telling* to sum up our ideas, clear out the clutter of too many details, and prevent our readers from losing sight of the main point. But a little specificity is important. So we try to select just those few details that enable us to plant a solid image in their minds.

"A major purpose of the ladder of abstraction, then, is to help us decide how far up and down we need to climb to reach our readers at just the right rungs of generality and specificity. We keep the ladder upright by balancing our amounts of showing and telling. For instance, in a persuasive essay, I need to show just enough details for the reader to see my perspective, and enough telling to remind the reader of my main points and the truth as I see it."

"How do I know when enough is enough?" Jamie asked.

"Well, let's try something." Mrs. Flaherty turned to the empty ladder she had drawn on the board. "Why don't we start up here at the top with *Zeitgeist,* the topic of your history paper?"

"Okay."

Mrs. Flaherty wrote *Zeitgeist* next to a puffy cloud. "Now, think of a general statement that includes the word *Zeitgeist.* Maybe you can remember something you wrote in your paper."

"Hmmm. How about: Zeitgeist*, or the general set of thoughts and feelings characterizing today's youngest generation, is difficult to define.*"

"Wow. Sounds very vague! I don't know what you're talking about! Perfect!" Mrs. Flaherty was delighted.

Jamie wasn't sure if Mrs. Flaherty had complimented her or put her down.

"I mean," Mrs. Flaherty quickly explained at Jamie's look of dismay, "that you are going to have to climb down the ladder a bit to help me understand all the abstractions in that one sentence. The first question that pops into my mind is, 'What do you mean?'"

"I mean," Jamie tried to remember from her paper, "that in previous generations, people believed we could overcome the forces of nature, and that reason and technology could solve the world's problems. This was the Zeitgeist of the Modern era—from the late nineteenth century to the middle of the twentieth. But it didn't last."

"What do you mean? "Mrs. Flaherty repeated.

"Today, years after we thought reason and technology could solve everything, we've learned that excessive human consumption has depleted our planet's limited natural resources, and that the latest technologies have failed to save us from the forces of nature. In fact, we've used technology to plunder and destroy the world more than to protect and build it."

"Oh," said Mrs. Flaherty in a hollow voice, deflated by the force of Jamie's description. She wrote a summary on the rung below Zeitgeist: "*After a period of excessive human consumption and the depletion of natural resources, we realize that the latest technologies have been used to plunder and destroy the world…* You are certainly more specific, Jamie," she observed, "But can you be more so? What, exactly, do you mean by all of this? Notice how I have to keep asking, 'What exactly do you mean?' to force you down the ladder?"

Jamie felt that the challenge to be more specific was getting harder and harder to meet. "Well…," she thought about what she had written in her paper, "I think my generation has grown up with technology that can be used for many purposes—good and bad. For example, I go home to write a paper that is due the next day. I sit down at my computer to do research for it on the Internet. And I can type the paper up pretty quickly. If I make a mistake, I can go back and fix it in a second. My parents used to have to type everything on a typewriter. If they made mistakes, they had to white them out and type over them. What a pain that must have been!

"But at the same computer, I can spend three hours playing video games or looking for a cool pair of boots on Ebay—ones I'll never buy. At times, I feel so much better having swim practice or some after-school activity rather than going home and turning into a computer junkie.

"The problem is, I can't live without my computer, Mrs. Flaherty. It saves me so much time and puts me in touch with other people. But sometimes I think I use it to waste the time I just saved."

"So the computer helps you to save time and connect to the world in some ways, and to waste time and disconnect in other ways?" Mrs. Flaherty asked.

"Maybe that's it," Jamie wished she could have come up with these ideas in time for her paper on Zeitgeist. What great examples of how technology can build and destroy.

At the next step down the ladder, Mrs. Flaherty wrote *computer advantages and disadvantages* and Jamie's examples of each.

"Do you want to know next what I mean by all of that?" Jamie asked before Mrs. Flaherty could lower her chalk.

"You got it, Jamie. We're at the bottom rung of the ladder, and the time has come to *sense* what you are sensing at the computer. Can you describe what you see, hear, feel, taste, touch and even smell during these moments?"

Jamie closed her eyes and leaned back against her chair. "You want me to describe what I smell, too? The only smell that is coming to me is the lemon garlic chicken breasts roasting for dinner. My computer is in the kitchen. Wait! I can see myself reading an email from my cousin Natalie in California. She is my age, and unfortunately, we don't get to visit each other too often. I click on the link in her email, and suddenly—well, you have to understand Natalie's sense of humor, Mrs. Flaherty. She sends me a link to a cartoon of a pregnant-looking Santa Claus who smiles, sways back and forth, and farts to the tune of Jingle Bells while these little puffs of white smoke rise in the air around him. I laugh so hard my cheeks start to ache. And even though the cartoon is so silly, I get the warm, fuzzy feeling that my cousin is laughing along next to me."

"Very graphic," Mrs. Flaherty agreed.

Jamie opened her eyes. Her teacher was writing a list of descriptive words at the bottom of the ladder: *click, pregnant, smiles, sways, farts Jingle Bells, puffs of white smoke, rise, cheeks ache, warm, fuzzy.*"

"Wow. I really did it. I just described a concrete moment of Zeitgeist, Mrs. Flaherty. Didn't I show how my cousin was with me even though she was really in California? Santa Claus seemed real, too, even though he was just a cartoon. And I was hysterical over something he'd do in the bathroom! In my paper on Zeitgeist, I wrote that the spirit of my age has to do with the simulation of reality, the blurring of time and space and the illusion of being in more than one place at the same time. Also, my friends and I are a generation of eavesdroppers—we delight in watching what used to be said and done behind closed doors. My mother once said she was so busy she had to satisfy her need for girlfriends by watching reruns of *Sex in the City*."

"If this is your description of moments of connection, what do moments of *dis*connection feel like?" Mrs. Flaherty was curious.

"That's easy. When I am disconnected from the world—and even from myself—I don't think I see, hear, taste, touch, feel, or smell much of anything. I'm a dangler in the cyberspace of my computer; I'm a zombie glued to the screen. I live for the sole purpose of getting to the next level of some game, zapping the dark-suited villains before they zap me. Whether I survive the forces of evil or not, I want to keep going. What seems like a few minutes turns into hours. Suddenly, it's dinnertime and I haven't touched my homework or helped to set the table in spite of my mom's repeated naggings."

"Hmmm. Disconnection on one level, but perhaps connection on another." Mrs. Flaherty's gaze seemed to penetrate a hole in Jamie's forehead. "So what are the concrete words you used to describe this aspect of Zeitgeist?" she asked, chalk poised in midair.

Jamie struggled to remember what she had just said. The words were still there: "*Dangler, zombie, glued to the screen, zapping, dark-suited villains?*"

"Good!" Mrs. Flaherty quickly filled the remaining space at the lowest rung of the ladder. "This is more helpful to me than you know, Jamie. You described my kids on the computer. I can now begin to imagine what is going on inside their heads. Now tell me, did you climb up and down the Ladder of Abstraction in your paper on Zeitgeist? Did you show and tell, and tell and show? Did you keep the ladder balanced by going up then down then up?"

"I didn't get to the bottom of the ladder, " Jamie admitted. "I stopped at the rung describing our *Zeitgeist* as the simulation of reality."

"Not bad, Jamie. But as your reader, I would need to *feel* the Zeitgeist to connect with you on a deeper level. If you had selected a few of these sensory words like *Jingle Bells* or *puffs of white smoke* to help immerse me in your experience, your essay would leave on me a more lasting impression. Now," Mrs. Flaherty said as she eyed her watch, "Let's rewrite this lesson on the ladder of abstraction and look at some more examples in time for you to make the late bus."

"Now it's my turn. What do *you* mean?" Jamie asked.

Mrs. Flaherty laughed. "I mean that I think we can try replacing our 'ladder' with something familiar to your experience—something that you do on a more frequent basis. Do you climb ladders as much as you use your computer?"

"No. Not *real* ladders, anyway," Jamie replied.

"Huh?" Mrs. Flaherty asked.

"Well, when I search the Web for information, it's kind of like climbing up and down a ladder. I start out by typing in key words to come up with links to websites on my topic. If my key words are too general, I come up with links remotely related to my topic. For example, when I had to write a paper on imagery for language arts, I came up with tons of links to geospatial intelligence. Once I learned more about my topic, I started plugging in specific key words and finding more relevant information. But sometimes, when I am *too* specific, my search might bring up nothing—zero results."

"That's another excellent way to look at moving from general to specific," Mrs. Flaherty agreed. "In much the same way, if I had too much telling and not enough showing in my essay, the reader could interpret what I'm trying to say very broadly and maybe miss my meaning entirely. On the other hand, too much showing and not enough telling might overwhelm my readers with too much detail and cause them to lose sight of my point. The right balance of showing and telling is what works best."

"Is there a trick to finding the best balance?" Jamie was still not sure how to determine just the right amount of showing and telling.

"Well, think back to the question that I asked you over and over when you were describing Zeitgeist."

"You mean, *what do you mean?*" Jamie replied.

"Precisely. How many times did I ask you, '*What do you mean?*' before I could sense what Zeitgeist was all about to you?"

Jamie tried to recall. "Four times?" she guessed.

"Close! I asked you three times, and you asked yourself the last time, remember?"

"So I have to ask myself, '*What do I mean?*' four times before I get to the right level of detail?" Jamie was incredulous.

"Maybe. On average, three to five times, depending on how general a statement you start out with. Let's try it, Jamie. You say *every cloud has a silver lining*. What do you really mean by that?" Mrs. Flaherty held up her index finger and mouthed *one*.

"I mean an experience can start out as a negative one but end up being positive."

"And what do you mean by that?" Mrs. Flaherty held up two fingers.

Jamie felt distracted by the countdown. "Uh, well, something negative like my parents' divorce turned into a learning experience for us all."

"What do you mean by that?"

"Well, I remember the lessons I learned from my parents' divorce. They are on my Gears Map." Jamie felt recharged. "Let's see... My family expanded and I developed new relationships. I became closer to my brother. My parents actually changed for the better. I was forced to take on new responsibilities."

"Okay. But what do you mean?" Mrs. Flaherty repeated, holding up four fingers.

"What?" Jamie asked. "If I were writing an essay in twenty-five minutes, I couldn't get to all of them. Maybe two or three at the most."

"Good point," Mrs. Flaherty agreed. How about stick to one lesson, *my parents actually changed for the better*. What do you mean by that one? The word 'better' is pretty abstract to me, your reader."

"My Mom always used to depend on my Dad to do the dirty work. He took out the garbage and fixed the toilet. He paid all the bills. When a problem came up, my mom would shrug her shoulders and say, '*You figure it out, Jim. That's your job.*' After the separation, she finally realized she had to stop calling him every time something went wrong. She learned how to do her own taxes. Now she's a regular at Home Depot."

"A regular at Home Depot? What do you mean?" Mrs. Flaherty held up five fingers in triumph. "Make this the ground level!" she reminded Jamie. "Give me detail! Draw me into your experience! I want to connect *here*!" She pounded her fist over her heart.

"Okay." Jamie took a deep breath. Mrs. Flaherty was scaring her. "One night a few months ago, I woke up to all this banging and clattering. I didn't know what to think. Was a burglar in our kitchen? Or did another raccoon find the hole in our attic and decide to explore the cupboard full of pots and pans? I crept down the long hallway to the kitchen, clutching my lacrosse stick just in case, while the banging turned into this strange ripping sound. When I peeked into the kitchen, I gasped. Not at a burglar or wild animal, but at the sight of boxes and cans strewn all over the floor and counters, and a gaping hole in one wall.

"There my Mom stood, with a hammer over her head. She was about to crash it into the pantry. 'Mom!' I screamed. She must have jumped higher than the sink. By the time she landed and saw the look on my face, she knew I needed an explanation. 'I—I couldn't sleep, dear,' she smiled sweetly, 'and I thought we might be able to put a little office space in here.' Home Depot has created a monster."

Mrs. Flaherty laughed. "Excellent showing! I could see your mother about to attack the wall with her hammer."

"By the way, that's how we ended up with a place in the kitchen for our computer. It worked out well. It's probably what helped our house to sell so quickly. Would you like to hear the story about the time my mom had to jumpstart her car all by herself?" Jamie was just getting started.

"I'd love to… but we don't have time. And showing does take time. What I'd like you to do instead is to take this piece of paper, Jamie, and capture that story of your mother's kitchen demolition in one to three sentences at the most."

"That's so hard!" Jamie protested.

"But entirely possible." Mrs. Flaherty assured her. "What few words would be enough to show your reader that striking picture of your mother?"

In spite of her resistance, Jamie dashed off a description. "Okay. How's this?" She read: *"The night I woke up to find my mother in the kitchen about to crash a sledge hammer into our pantry wall, I realized even the storm cloud of divorce had a silver lining. Before she separated from my father, my mother would avoid changing a light bulb. Now she was shopping at Home Depot, tearing down walls, and creating an airy kitchen out of the ruins of a cluttered closet."*

Mrs. Flaherty smiled. "That's quite a hook, Jamie."

"Hook?" Jamie echoed.

"On some level, you must have felt like you were writing your essay. You hooked your reader with a vivid image of your mother ready to destroy the pantry, then shifted to your insight about the silver lining in divorce, and illustrated that insight with the contrast between your mother who wasn't very handy before the divorce, but became a regular at Home Depot afterwards. You went from showing to telling to a blend of showing and telling. You even threw in another metaphor at the end—just as clouds can have silver linings, cluttered closets can be transformed into airy kitchens. I guess there is life after divorce!"

Jamie was surprised she could capture so much meaning in one minute and three sentences. "Do you think I could write like this on the SAT essay?" she asked.

"Why not? You quite naturally climbed up and down the Ladder of Abstraction. All in less than one paragraph. You have it in you, Jamie."

Jamie was in awe of her own power. Perhaps Dorothy in The Wizard of Oz felt this way when she discovered she could have returned home to Kansas all along. All that she had to do was click together her ruby red slippers three times.

"You have discovered something very powerful, Jamie." Mrs. Flaherty, as usual, showed her uncanny ability to read into Jamie's thoughts. "Showing is an effective way to grab your reader's attention at the beginning of your essay. You started out with an image of your mother, and immediately enabled your reader to connect with you on a sensory level.

"It is no accident that the best techniques for hooking your reader are also techniques of showing or illustrating your experience. Just as last week

I gave you examples of telling; this week, I am going to send you on your way with examples of showing. Your assignment is to read through these examples and find ones of your own to illustrate each technique. My hope is, as you get really good at showing and telling, you will learn not only how to move from one to the other, but also, to blend the two and use more than one technique in a single essay sentence or paragraph."

Mrs. Flaherty picked up a packet from the pile on her desk. "And to reinforce what we've learned about moving from general to specific, I'm going to give you some worksheets on climbing up and down the Ladder of Abstraction. It would be a tremendous help to me, Jamie, if you could create for my students and me a worksheet on moving from general to specific by using your own example."

"Hmmm. I'll try." That was all Jamie could promise at this point. Her mind was on something else. "I feel really good right now!" she marveled. "Maybe it is because I wrote that hook."

"Maybe!" Mrs. Flaherty squeezed Jamie's shoulder as she presented her with the weekly handouts. "Writing can be fun and make you feel really good—like Dorothy going home to Kansas."

Later the next evening, Jamie reviewed her handouts and using the hook she had written in her meeting with Mrs. Flaherty, produced a handout of her own.

Climbing Down the Ladder of Abstraction

Moving from the general to the specific:

GENERAL	Predator
MORE SPECIFIC	Marine Carnivorous Fish
MORE SPECIFIC	Shark
MORE SPECIFIC	Mackerel Shark
MOST SPECIFIC	Great White Shark

GENERAL	Mass Media
MORE SPECIFIC	Newspaper
MORE SPECIFIC	Financial Newspaper
MORE SPECIFIC	Wall Street Journal
MOST SPECIFIC	December 19, 2005 issue of the Wall Street Journal

GENERAL	Writing
MORE SPECIFIC	Play
MORE SPECIFIC	Broadway Musical
MOST SPECIFIC	*The Lion King*

Moving from the abstract to the concrete:

ABSTRACT	Renaissance culture
MORE CONCRETE	Italian Renaissance art
MORE CONCRET	Florentine Renaissance Sculpture
MOST CONCRETE	Michelangelo's David

ABSTRACT	Communication
MORE CONCRETE	Stone inscribed with symbols
MORE CONCRETE	Ancient stone inscribed with writing system symbols discovered in 18th Century Egypt
MORE CONCRETE	Ancient stone inscribed with Egyptian Hieroglyphics discovered in 18th Century Egypt
MOST CONCRETE	Rosetta Stone

ABSTRACT	Nutrition
MORE CONCRETE	Diet Food
MORE CONCRETE	Diet Food Drink
MOST CONCRETE	Slim-fast brand High Protein Creamy Strawberry Shake

FROM TELLING (GENERAL/ABSTRACT) TO SHOWING (SPECIFIC/CONCRETE): TECHNIQUES FOR CLIMBING DOWN THE LADDER OF ABSTRACTION

1. **Illustrations/Sensory Details** allow your readers to see, touch, hear, taste, smell, and feel what your ideas, images, and experiences are like.

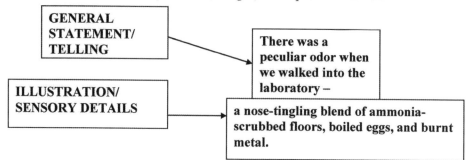

There was a peculiar odor when we walked into the laboratory – a nose-tingling blend of ammonia-scrubbed floors, boiled eggs, and burnt metal.

2. **Explanations/elaborations** enable your readers to grasp more fully the meaning of your point or idea.

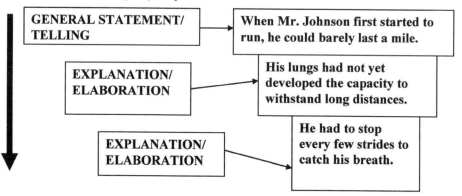

When Mr. Johnson first started to run, he could barely last a mile. His lungs had not yet developed the capacity to withstand lo ng distances. He had to stop every few strides to catch his breath.

3. **Facts/verifiable details** offer your readers the concrete particulars of your idea. Facts can help convince your reader of the validity of your argument.

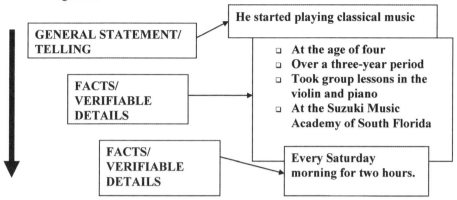

He started playing classical music at the age of four. Over a three-year period, he took group lessons in the violin and piano at the Suzuki Music Academy of South Florida every Saturday morning for two hours.

4. **Comparisons/Contrasts** enable the reader to see your object or idea next to a similar or dissimilar one.

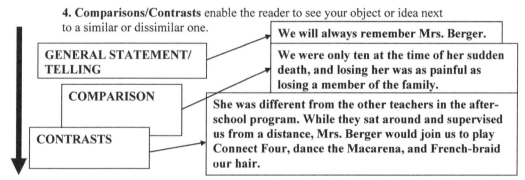

We will always remember Mrs. Berger. We were only ten at the time of her sudden death, and losing her was as painful as losing a member of the family. She was different from the other teachers in the after-school program. While they sat around and supervised us from a distance, Mrs. Berger would join us to play Connect Four, dance the Macarena, and French-braid our hair.

5. **Creative or humorous details** trigger a smile, sense of bonding, warmth, wonder, or curiosity in the reader.

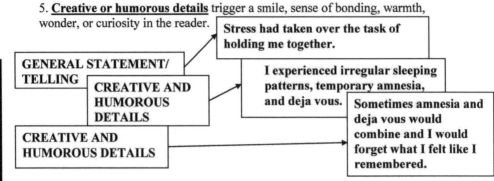

Stress had taken over the task of holding me together. I experienced irregular sleeping patterns, temporary amnesia and deja vous. Sometimes amnesia and deja vous would combine and I would forget what I felt like I remembered.
Ben Ouyang, West Windsor Plainsboro High School

6. **Action details** carry the reader into the heart of action and enhance the momentum of your argument. The use of powerful, precise verbs might actually cause the reader's muscles to tense.

```
GENERAL STATEMENT/      →  I doubted we would survive the final
TELLING                    ascent – the last 100 feet of Pike's
                           Rock.
    ACTION              →  She clenched my hand…
    DETAILS
ACTION                  →  Although my body cried to let go, I forced every
DETAILS                    last ounce of strength into my fingers and
                           strained to hold on.
```

I doubted we would survive the final ascent – the last 100 feet of Pike's Rock. She clenched my hand, nearly cutting of my circulation. Although my body cried to let go, I forced every last ounce of strength into my fingers and strained to hold on.

7. Metaphors or analogies enable the reader to quickly grasp a complex idea or topic. The reader can connect to the writer's idea or experience by relating it to a similar symbol, image, or object or to a parallel experience.

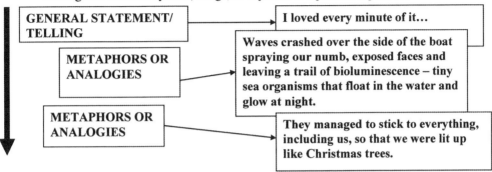

I loved every minute of it... Waves crashed over the side of the boat spraying our numb, exposed faces and leaving a trail of bioluminescence – tiny sea organisms that float in the water and glow at night. They managed to stick to everything, including us, so that we were lit up like Christmas trees.
Kelsey Johnson, West Windsor Plainsboro High School

8. Inner thoughts expose the writer's natural voice and unique way of thinking, enabling the reader to observe from an inside perspective.

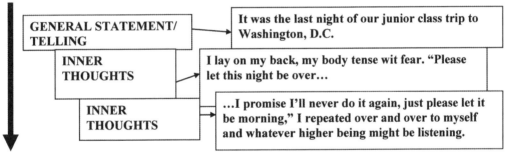

It was the last night of our junior class trip to Washington, D.C. I lay on my back, my body tense with fear. "Please let this night be over. I promise I'll never do it again, just please let it be morning," I repeated over and over to myself and whatever higher being might be listening.
Kelsey Johnson, West Windsor Plainsboro High School

9. **Quotations** enable the reader to grasp the essence of the writer's message through the sayings of respected and trusted masters on the topic. If not overly wordy, obtuse, or clichéd, quotations can be an effective way to set the stage for or conclude an essay.

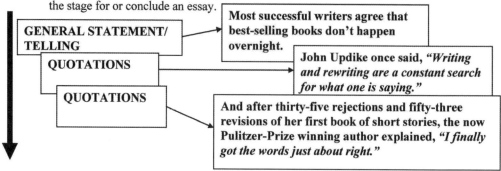

Most successful writers agree that best-selling books don't happen overnight. John Updike once said, "Writing and rewriting are a constant search for what one is saying." And after thirty-five rejections and fifty-three revisions of her first book of short stories, the now Pulitzer-Prize winning author explained, "I finally got the words just about right."

10. **Dialogue** draws the reader into the naturally engaging process of conversation.

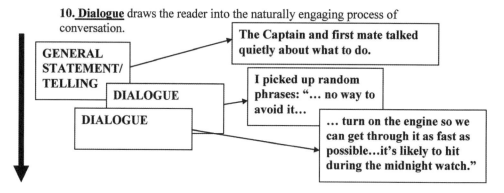

The Captain and first mate talked quietly about what to do. I picked up random phrases: "... no way to avoid it... turn on the engine so we can get through it as fast as possible...it's likely to hit during the midnight watch."
Kelsey Johnson, West Windsor Plainsboro High School

11. <u>Insights</u> enable the reader to identify with or learn from your deep, sometimes sudden understanding of a situation and your intuitions about the inner nature of things.

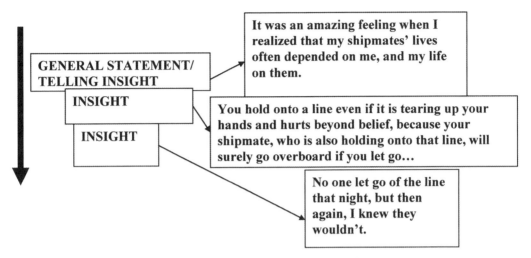

It was an amazing feeling to realize that my shipmates' lives often depended on me, and my life on them. You hold onto a line even if it is tearing up your hands and hurts beyond belief, because your shipmate, who is also holding onto that line, will surely go overboard if you let go... No one let go of the line that night, but then again, I knew they wouldn't.
Kelsey Johnson, West Windsor Plainsboro High School

DEEPENING THE LEVEL OF ENGAGEMENT:
By Jamie

Level I: GENERAL — ...I realized that even the storm cloud of divorce had a silver lining. — *Conclusion/Insight/Metaphor*

Level II: MORE SPECIFIC — The night I woke up to find my mother in the kitchen about to crash a sledge hammer into our pantry wall... — *Action/Sensory Details*

Level III: MORE SPECIFIC — Before she separated from my father, my mother had trouble changing a light bulb. Now she was shopping at Home Depot, tearing down walls, and creating an airy kitchen out of the ruins of a cluttered closet. — *Contrasts/Action Details*

The night I woke up to find my mother in the kitchen about to crash a sledge hammer into our pantry wall, I realized that even the storm cloud of divorce had a silver lining. Before she separated from my father, my mother had trouble changing a light bulb. Now she was shopping at Home Depot, tearing down walls, and creating an airy kitchen out of the ruins of a cluttered closet.

Chapter Thirteen

Tie Your Ideas Together: Smooth Transitioning

"Mrs. Flaherty!" Jamie entered the room in a daze of disbelief.

The language arts teacher looked up from a curious mountain of fabric scraps and spools of thread strewn across her desk.

"Mr. Dillon likes my *Zeitgeist* paper so much, he wants me to shorten it and submit it to the *Your Turn* Student Essay competition," Jamie announced. "It's a national contest with a first prize of $5000."

Mrs. Flaherty smiled. "Congratulations! I'm not surprised at all, Jamie. When you talked about your paper last week, I could tell you had done an excellent job on it. I'd love to see it when you're ready. If you don't mind, I'd even like to use it as an example for my students."

"That reminds me," Jamie said. "I wrote the handout you asked for on Levels of Engagement."

While Mrs. Flaherty examined Jamie's handout, Jamie examined the squares of felt and cotton on her teacher's desk.

"I give up," Jamie admitted. "What's all this stuff? How are we going to find your dictionary today?"

"Excellent!" Mrs. Flaherty exclaimed, ignoring Jamie's remark. "I actually prefer your terms, *deepening the level of engagement* over *climbing down the ladder of abstraction*. If it's okay with you, I'm going to redo my handouts with this new way of thinking about how to get from general to specific."

"Sure! Uh, Mrs. Flaherty?" Jamie pointed at the mountain of scraps.

"What?" Mrs. Flaherty acted as if she barely noticed anything out of the ordinary. "Ah—that." She patted the top layer of her pile. "Just a little idea I had for teaching my students about transitions—you know, the *T* in WRITE: *Transition smoothly between ideas and paragraphs.*

"Here." Mrs. Flaherty carefully selected five patches of material from the pile and handed them to Jamie. "And take this needle and thread."

Jamie accepted the items, uncertain about what to do with them.

"I'm still trying to get the metaphor just right, Jamie. So please bear with me," Mrs. Flaherty explained. "I want you to imagine that each of those five pieces of material is a distinct paragraph of your SAT essay. As a matter of fact, if you were looking closely, you would notice labels on the material. *Introduction. Body Paragraph #1. Body Paragraph #2. Body Paragraph #3.* And *Conclusion.*"

"Yep, I see them," Jamie said, automatically ordering the scraps in the formulaic sequence of the typical five-paragraph essay.

"You see, the paragraphs are not joined together in any way. Now, imagine that the thread in your hand is all you have to hold your essay together. Go ahead. You have two minutes to connect your paragraphs. I don't care how neatly or sloppily you sew the pieces together, as long as you abide by three rules: first, use only one piece of unbroken thread; second, connect the squares in such a way that they aren't stacked directly on top of each other, but instead, like a train with couplers between the cars; and third, connect each square in the right order.

"In other words," Mrs. Flaherty cautioned, "You want to be sure to start with the intro and end with the conclusion—be careful not to sew them between the body paragraphs or anything out of order like that."

Two minutes later, Jamie smoothed her creation on a desk. Once satisfied, she picked it up by the introduction piece and dangled it in the air. It looked like the fabric mobile over the crib of the little girl she babysat down the street.

"I did it, Mrs. Flaherty. But I still don't get it."

Mrs. Flaherty rose from her desk to admire Jamie's handiwork. "Hmmm. Notice how you had to run some stitches not only between the paragraphs, but inside of them as well."

"Otherwise I would've had too much thread lying slack and the squares would have bunched up together." Jamie, who rarely in her life had picked up a needle and thread, defended her sewing. "I had to sew stitches through each square to make the whole train lie flat."

"Makes sense. The reason I asked you to do this, Jamie, is that I think of transitions as the thread tying together the ideas of your essay. Remember, I said the thread had to be unbroken. In much the same way, when you write an essay, you should run a continuous thread of transitions through it from start to finish. The second you break that thread, or jump to a new idea without linking it to the last, your entire argument could unravel, and you could lose the underlying tension of your essay."

Jamie was starting to see more connections between the sewing metaphor and writing with transitions. Her Mom's sewing machine had a special knob on it to adjust the tension of the thread. If she turned it too much in one direction, the thread got tight and broke. If she turned it too much the other way, the seam loosened and fell apart.

"I never really used to think much about transitions," Jamie confessed. "I'll probably think about them more from now on, though. Not many teachers give us a needle and thread to get their *point* across!"

"Hold on. I'm not done yet." Mrs. Flaherty chuckled, getting Jamie's pun. "I also asked you to avoid stacking the squares on top of each other, and to connect them in the proper sequence."

"Okay," Jamie tried to decipher Mrs. Flaherty's remaining rules. "Maybe you wanted to make sure the squares—I mean paragraphs—were separated, with a thread or transition between them, rather than five squares stacked on top of each other like one big paragraph."

Mrs. Flaherty pulled a student's essay from beneath the scraps and held it out to Jamie. "You mean like this?" she asked. A large, unbroken paragraph covered the entire page.

"Whoa!" Jamie said, startled. The paragraph seemed like a huge wall of words. "It makes me tired just looking at it! Shouldn't I at least be able to see a beginning, middle and end before I start to read the essay?"

"This is what I call an 'unfriendly'-looking essay. I can guess before reading it the student probably threw too many ideas into one paragraph. Transitions would have helped him to separate each idea into its own paragraph but keep these ideas tied together. You're right, Jamie. This essay would look a lot more inviting to the reader if we could distinguish a beginning, middle, and end to it.

"Your creation over there," Mrs. Flaherty gestured toward the mobile, "is the product of an experiment. An experiment in what it actually takes to hold an essay together. Imagine you are up to the concluding phase of your learning cycle. What else have you learned about writing transitions from sewing together five squares of fabric with one piece of thread?"

"Well," Jamie thought aloud, "you yourself noticed I had to run a few stitches from one corner of each square to the opposite corner, and then connect that point to the point of the next square with a couple of tight stitches to hold the squares together. Otherwise, the squares would have hung too loosely and they would have folded up at the middle.

"Maybe I need to do the same kind of thing when I write my essay. Usually, I only worry about transitions *between* paragraphs. But I need to think about how to make my writing flow more smoothly inside paragraphs, too. By running the thread—or writing transitions—between words and sentences in the paragraph, my argument would sound less bumpy. I wouldn't be jumping around so much from one idea to another, or just throwing a bunch of ideas about my topic together without connecting them."

"Great, Jamie. I'd say we're ready for the applying phase of the learning cycle. The how-to's of tightening your argument with a continuous thread of transitions. First, though, I have an important point to add here. A point about sewing squares together with a needle and thread, and about tying ideas together with transitions." Mrs. Flaherty pointed to Jamie's string of squares.

"Notice most of your stitches are directly visible. You've done some nice, traditional stitching in straight rows. The words you use to flow from one idea to the next are examples of traditional transitional expressions—like *but, furthermore, therefore,* and so on. I'll show you more examples of these direct kinds of transitions in a couple of minutes. My favorite transitions, however, are less direct and obvious. They aren't as visible as these stitches. But they're there. They involve a more subtle use of words, phrases, and techniques to thread your argument together in a seamless way. Imagine sewing with invisible thread, or sewing inside the cloth so your stitching can't be seen on the surface."

"I'm not sure I ever really learned how to do that." Jamie remarked. She could have been talking about sewing or writing.

"It's a lifelong art," her teacher sighed. "But one that'll come more naturally to you with a little practice. So first let's take a look at the more direct, traditional kinds of transitions. The blatantly obvious ones. Then we'll look at the more subtle types of transition."

Mrs. Flaherty slipped her hands underneath the mountain on her desk, feeling her way to a stack of handouts, while Jamie lunged to catch the pieces of material spilling onto the floor.

"Notice, Jamie," Mrs. Flaherty explained as she handed Jamie a booklet, "the first page describes the purpose of transitions, then shows the impact transitions can have on the interpretation of a sentence. The following pages define the different types of transitions, show how they're used, and give examples. Between now and our meeting next week, review these examples and come up with your own for each type of transition.

"If you don't have any examples from essays you've already written," Mrs. Flaherty continued, "make up new ones. You'll like that! Be sure to observe how some of these transitions are pretty subtle. As you become more effective at using transitions, I bet you'll find yourself choosing the 'seamless,' subtle type more than the traditional, direct transitional expressions."

Over the next few days, Jamie reviewed the handouts on the following pages and practiced using the different types of transitional expressions in her writing.

Transitions: The Thread that Holds Your Essay Together

Think of transitions as the thread of words and phrases that unifies the points of your argument, guides your reader through your writing, and ties your essay into a cohesive whole. Transitions are, in fact, the direct or subtle cues you provide so that your reader can understand the relationships between your ideas. They are the expressions that smooth and clarify the progression of your thinking.

Writing with a continuous thread of transitions, then, is what enables your reader to absorb your train of thought. In contrast, writing that lacks such a thread can cause the reader to derail or lose track of your central meaning.

In summary, my final advice to emerging writers is this: *Avoid presenting an argument that is too abrupt, choppy, and confusing for your reader to follow. Instead, master the use of transitions—the thread that holds your essay together and keeps the reader aboard your train of thought.*

How Transitions Can Clarify the Relationship Between Ideas

Consider these two sentences:

The doctor prescribed a new medication. The patient's condition took a turn for the worse.

What is the relationship between the doctor's prescribing a new medication and the patient's condition taking a turn for the worse? Is the medication causing the turn for the worse? A transitional expression can clarify this relationship between ideas:

*The doctor prescribed a new medication; **as a result**, the patient's condition took a turn for the worse.*

*The doctor prescribed a new medication **and** the patient's condition took a turn for the worse.*

*The doctor prescribed a new medication **in spite of the fact that** the patient's condition had taken a turn for the worse.*

*The doctor prescribed a new medication **because** the patient's condition had taken a turn for the worse.*

*The doctor prescribed a new medication; **however**, the patient's condition had taken a turn for the worse.*

DIRECT TRANSITIONAL EXPRESSIONS

Words of Transition	How the Transition Clarifies the Relationship between Ideas	Purpose of the Transition	Example/s
for example after all an illustration of even for instance indeed in fact it is true of course specifically that is to illustrate as a case in point as an illustration in particular one such yet another namely to demonstrate	Ties an idea or paragraph to the next one by setting the stage for an example.	To provide a more specific illustration or example of your meaning.	*Great leaders are ones who aren't afraid to challenge the status quo. For example, Don Haskins, the Texas Western coach who was inducted to the Hall of Fame, led his all-black starting line-up to the NCAA Championship when basketball was largely a segregated sport.*
for instance to begin with in short specifically for example in other words certainly	Ties an idea or paragraph to the next one by setting the stage for an example, summary, explanation, or elaboration.	To explain, summarize, or elaborate on your meaning.	*We can listen at a rate of about 400 words per minute and speak at a rate of 120 – 180 words a minute. In other words, if we aren't paying close attention, we might hear only half of what someone is saying to us.*
indeed in fact as a matter of fact to be sure of course in any event by all means above all especially in particular most important surely	Reinforces the point of your idea or paragraph by setting the stage for a related point of emphasis.	To emphasize an idea or point.	*She loves women's basketball. In fact, she signed up for season tickets one year in advance.*

Words of Transition		How the Transition Clarifies the Relationship between Ideas	Purpose of the Transition	Example/s
likewise similarly in the same way in the same equally	also as well both neither along the same lines manner	Accentuates the similarity between two ideas by setting the stage for one or more points of comparison.	To show comparison or similarity.	Mrs. Arlin spends at least an hour selecting her wardrobe and putting her make up on each morning. She is often late to work. Similarly, her teenage daughter takes a great deal of time getting ready for school and frequently misses the bus.
however even though on the other hand nevertheless although and yet but despite even so for all that in contrast	in spite of notwithstanding on the contrary regardless still though yet be that as it may whereas but at the same time	Accentuates the difference between two ideas by setting the stage for one or more points of contrast.	To show comparison or contrast.	Adam spent his childhood years as a ward of the State of Alabama. Although initially he had no family to call his own, he grew up to be a loving father of six and foster parent to countless homeless children over the years.
another related to furthermore also moreover further besides too and then again and then next finally still	too besides and as well besides beyond that first (second, third, last) for one thing what is more equally important in addition to	Ties an idea or paragraph to the next one by setting the stage to present additional related points.	To present additional related ideas.	To listen carefully, we must first devote our undivided attention to the speaker. We must absorb what he or she says in words and also conveys through tone of voice and body language. Second, we must be aware of our own biases that might filter our perceptions of the speaker's story.

Words of Transition		How the Transition Clarifies the Relationship between Ideas	Purpose of the Transition	Example/s
therefore thus as a result of consequently hence accordingly because for this purpose otherwise since then thereupon to this end		Ties a cause to its effect.	To show cause and effect.	*From the start of the season, she practiced kicking soccer balls into the goal every day for one to two hours. Therefore, when the coach had to select a line up of penalty kickers for the State championship game, her name was first on the list.*
finally in short in other words in a word to sum up in conclusion in the end all in all altogether in brief in other words	in particular in short in simpler terms in summary in sum on the whole that is therefore to put it differently to summarize	Ties an idea or set of ideas to points of summary or conclusion.	To conclude.	*In sum, the team had the "winningest" season in school history.*
first second in the first place last moreover next finally		Ties one idea or paragraph to the next by indicating the particular order or progression between them.	To show sequence.	*In the first place, the driver shouldn't have left the scene of the accident before the police arrived. Moreover, he should have left his contact information with the driver of the car that he hit. Finally, he should have realized that several bystanders bore witness to his role in the crash and wrote down his license plate number.*

Tie Your Ideas Together: Smooth Transitioning

Words of Transition		How the Transition Clarifies the Relationship between Ideas	Purpose of the Transition	Example/s
certainly granted that of course no doubt to be sure		To tie an idea to a point of concession.	To concede a point.	*The teacher was thorough in her presentation of the types of plagiarism. Of course, she was careful to avoid using students' examples of plagiarism before acquiring their permission.*
above adjacent to below elsewhere farther on here near nearby on the other side opposite to	to the east to the left in front in the foreground in the back in the background at the side adjacent nearby in the distance there	To tie one idea to the next by indicating the spatial relationship between them.	To show place.	*The sleepy town rested on the shores of Sturgeon Lake. Five miles to the east, the research team from the University opened a satellite office and launched their study on frog mutations.*
either/or neither/nor on the other hand instead of		To tie an idea to its alternative.	To show alternative.	*Neither the teacher nor the students were able to comprehend the tragedy.*
provided that if unless		To tie one idea to the next by indicating their conditional relationship.	To show condition, meaning that something will happen only if something else happens first.	*All applicants should show up at the interview center at the time, date, and room indicated on the poster unless they have been personally notified of their acceptance to or rejection from the program.*

Words of Transition		How the Transition Clarifies the Relationship between Ideas	Purpose of the Transition	Example/s
afterward as long as as soon as at last at length at that time before earlier formerly immediately in the meantime in the past lately later meanwhile while now presently shortly simultaneously since so far soon subsequently	then thereafter until until now when soon after previously at length next eventually after awhile at present briefly currently during finally first, (second, and so on) gradually in the future now recently suddenly	To tie one idea to the next by indicating the temporal relationship between them.	To show time, place in time, or the passage of time.	*While the students were busy preparing for the senior prom, their parents were spending long hours in the high school's auditorium setting up for the post-prom party.*
as because for since		To tie an idea to its underlying reason.	To give a reason.	*He was picked up by the local police because they found him sleeping on the beach after the senior prom.*
as though as if		To tie an idea or action to the manner or way in which it occurs.	To show manner.	*The principal interpreted the criticism as though it were a personal affront to his character.*

SEAMLESS TRANSITIONS

Words of Transition	How the Transition Clarifies the Relationship between Ideas	Purpose of the Transition	Example/s
sometimes frequently occasionally often	To tie an idea or action to the frequency or degree to which it occurs.	To show frequency.	*The student frequently took advantage of the teacher's extra-help sessions.*
these this those that	To tie back to a previous thing or idea, or refer to a current or future thing or idea by replacing it with a demonstrative pronoun.	To show spatial relationship*; or to refer to a previous, current or future thing or idea**.	* *I'd like to explain this essay, not that one in the next chapter.* ***These moments are the ones we will remember for years to come.* ***These are the times when we need to try even harder to understand.* ** *Courage, initiative, compassion and respect for others – these are the qualities we want in a genuine leader.*
his her it its they their theirs	To tie back to a previous thing, person, category or idea, or refer to a current or future thing, person, category or idea by replacing it with a personal or possessive pronoun, or with the word/s: "one/s".	To refer to a previous, current or future thing, person, category or idea.	*Doris faded to the back of the crowd and slipped out the door. Only Jack knew that* she *was the* one *who had come up with the successful plan.* *He chose the long circuitous route instead of the short direct* one. *Although the* Yale *research team* created the theory, *the reporter failed to mention that the original idea* was theirs.

Words of Transition	How the Transition Clarifies the Relationship between Ideas	Purpose of the Transition	Example/s
Repetition of key words.	To continue developing or elaborating on a previous thing or idea by repeating it verbatim.	To show continued development of or elaboration on a specific idea.	*The movie was filmed in the rural landscape of southern France. The landscape was dotted by groves of olive trees and field after field of grapevines.* *He is not exceptionally handsome. He avoids celebrations of his fame and fortune. He wears turtlenecks and polyester jeans.* *He is the new breed of sheik geek. With a few brief churnings of his brilliant mind and one dark-eyed glance, he can stop his opponents in their tracks and sweep women off their feet.*
Paraphrases, summary words or phrases.	To tie together sentences and/or paragraphs by paraphrasing or summarizing the previous idea/s in a concise word or phrase.	To continue the development of a main idea.	*First, her water broke. Then, the abdominal pains struck at irregular intervals. Finally, the pains arrived one after the other in quick succession until she was fully dilated.* *The entire process of labor took 72 minutes.*
Paraphrases, summary words or phrases.	To set the stage for an upcoming idea by summarizing it in a concise word or phrase.	To continue the development of a main idea.	*A host of factors contributed to the storm's tragic effects.* *First, it was Super Bowl Sunday. Hundreds of people were glued to their TV's but oblivious to the stream of weather advisories flashing across their screens. Second, …*
Repetition or paraphrases of the essay's main purpose.	To tie ideas together by reminding the reader of their connection to the essay's main purpose.	To develop a central argument.	*Aaron's family consisted of one biological sister, two half-brothers, and a step-grandmother. Victor had arrived in this country with an older cousin as his guardian. Sheila just moved into her sixth foster home in three years. Rupert Moss, their teacher, had to quickly let go of his traditional notions of family.*

Tie Your Ideas Together: Smooth Transitioning

Words of Transition	How the Transition Clarifies the Relationship between Ideas	Purpose of the Transition	Example/s
Paraphrases, summary words or phrases.	To tie together ideas by beginning a new paragraph with a summary of or succinct reference to the main idea of the previous paragraph.	To continue the development of an idea or the progression of a central argument.	*It is already my second time playing the song when she stops me halfway through. At first I am annoyed, but she looks at me and says in a heavy Russian accent, "No Mamachica, you have the notes down but it is not music until you put your emotions into it." I smile. How can I not smile at this overly dramatic woman? I start to play again. This time the lady is swaying gently to the music with her eyes closed and singing in a rich vibrato voice. I laugh to myself while continuing to play. She is so odd and yet I somehow admire her.* *Her name is Glafira, but everyone calls her Lala…* Kelsey Johnson, West Windsor Plainsboro High School
Words of response.	To tie together ideas by posing a question at the end of one paragraph, and following up with the answer at the beginning of the next paragraph.	To continue the development of an idea or the progression of a central argument.	*What is the purpose of continuing to believe in Santa?* *According to newsman Francis Church, the world would otherwise be a dreary place. Without Santa, there would be no childlike faith, no poetry, no romance to make tolerable this existence.*

Chapter Fourteen
Engage your Reader: Express your Voice Clearly

"Jamie," Mrs. Flaherty confided in her at their next meeting, "one of the most important things I've learned from all my years teaching writing is this: what we *think* we say in our writing is not necessarily what the reader understands from it. So much gets lost in translation. So much gets lost when we try to transfer the thoughts in our head to words on paper—words written clearly enough for the reader to fully get what we're trying to say."

Mrs. Flaherty seemed to have put her finger on what Jamie felt was the hardest thing about writing. "You're right, Mrs. Flaherty," she sighed. "Sometimes the idea might be really clear in my mind. But it sounds so mixed up by the time I write it. Why is that?" Jamie felt frustrated just thinking about it. "My friends complain too. They say their thoughts make sense in their heads but don't come out right on paper."

"Hmmm." Mrs. Flaherty nodded in commiseration. "So much stands in the way of finding just the right words to convey what we want to say. For starters, some of those great ideas we have stewing in our brains get lost before we ever capture them in words. After all, we think much faster than we write. I've heard that we think at a speed of about 400 to 500 words a minute when we're listening to others. Yet we write, on average, at about 20 to 30 words per minute if we're taking notes or writing from memory. So even if we have the sharpest of memories, we're bound to forget some of our ideas while we translate them to writing."

"Or," Mrs. Flaherty continued, "some of our ideas make it to paper all right, but the words and ways we choose to express them end up being too confusing or vague for the reader to understand. *We* understand what we are trying to say. But how often do we read our own writing from our reader's perspective? How often do we get a true sense of how our words are perceived by others? The readers' perception of our writing is what ultimately determines its effectiveness. Our readers are the gauge of how well we write, and they might find our words confusing or vague."

Mrs. Flaherty rose from her desk and walked over to Jamie, who was sitting in her usual seat in the front row. Jamie could swear her teacher's eyes were misted over. For a second, Jamie felt her own frustration must have been contagious.

"So all this leads us to the *E* in *write*?" Jamie asked, trying to stay on task in spite of the unexpected tide of emotion stirring inside her. Coupled with her frustration, she knew this was her last session with Mrs. Flaherty. They had reached the final letter of their *think to write, write to think* strategy. The SAT was two weeks away. She knew she had learned a lot, but also knew she had so much more to learn.

Jamie struggled to maintain her composure as a wave of sadness continued to swell in her chest, threatening to swallow her voice. Quickly, she cleared her throat, blinked hard, and forced herself to speak. Her voice had a strange, hoarse quality to it as if someone else were talking.

"I want to be a writer, Mrs. Flaherty. Even though my writing can be painful and take forever and not make any sense, I still want to write. But I'm afraid after all of your teaching and Mr. Johnson's coaching on how to manage my anxiety, I'm still not that good. Plus, I'll still get a low grade on the SAT essay. I might not be able to get out what I know is inside of me in 25 minutes. Some woman in Iowa who rates essays will end up with mine and think I can't put a sentence together. She'll give me a *one* or a *two*. Little will she know she's grading a person who will someday write a book on Oprah Winfrey's book list. I just need more time, Mrs. Flaherty. I need more time to get good at this."

Jamie couldn't tell if Mrs. Flaherty was laughing so hard she was crying or if she was crying so hard she was laughing. "You'll be fine, Jamie." Mrs. Flaherty shook as she spoke. Her voice was full of a throaty, raw power that seemed to come from inside her chest. "You'll be *fine*," she repeated.

Jamie felt a funny sensation—as if her own voice was filling with power. She was confused. Instead of the wave of sadness she had been trying to suppress just a moment ago, she felt a wave of energy and warmth. The lump in her throat had melted. She looked at Mrs. Flaherty as if she were seeing her teacher in a new light. Was her teacher magical, after all?

Mrs. Flaherty cleared her throat. "You *are* a writer, Jamie. You have been from the day you were born. You always have a voice to express the truth about what you think and feel and do. Today, we'll talk about what gets in the way of your voice, and what'll help your readers more clearly understand what you are trying to say without losing much in translation."

Jamie nodded. She knew her voice wasn't all that clear to her readers.

"The *E* in write," Mrs. Flaherty continued, "is about *engaging* your reader by *expressing* your self in a way that is honest, forthright, and genuine. You want to find the right words to express the truth, your truth, clearly. Mastering some basic conventions of the modern English language is a great place to start. Sounds like a tall order to deliver over the next two weeks, but you can get a good start before the SAT. Engaging your reader by expressing your authentic voice is a goal you can continue to pursue long after the SAT is over."

"A tall order, all right." Jamie gulped. "So what gets in the way of expressing the truth?"

"Maybe the best thing to do is to show you rather than tell you," Mrs. Flaherty said, walking over to her desk. "I have some good examples of what gets in the way right here. Taken from student essays. Some of these examples are clear and concise—you can easily understand the ideas behind them—and other examples are hard to figure out."

"Okay." Jamie couldn't help but wonder if any of the examples were from her own essays. By now, her teacher must have a pretty large collection.

"First, Jamie, let's talk about what we mean by *clear*. How can we measure this quality?"

"I'm not sure," Jamie said. "But I know when I write something, I want my friends to be able to pick it up, read it, and understand it right away without having to read it over and over—like the Boring book I was telling you about last time we met."

"Hmmm. Keep in mind, Jamie, the average reader reads at about an eighth to tenth-grade reading level. That's what we reach by middle school and the first two years of high school—a very comfortable level to read at. The wider the audience, the more people you'll find at this level. Even if the subject you're writing about is complex, you can express it in a simple, uncluttered, easy-to-understand way to make it meaningful to this wider audience."

Mrs. Flaherty paused a moment for her words to sink in. "So let's talk about some of the writing habits I see in my students—the kinds of habits that prevent readers from understanding what my students are trying to say.

Mrs. Flaherty paused to give Jamie one of her long, searching looks. "I have a lot to show you in the next few minutes. Are you ready?"

Jamie eyed with amusement the pile of handouts Mrs. Flaherty had put on her desk. She nodded. "Let's get started. I've got to get this right."

Write clearly

"A key step to engage your reader is to write as clearly as possible. To do so," Mrs. Flaherty explained, "you must fight *wordiness* and overly flowery or 'fluffy' language, even though you might love it."

"Fluffy?" Jamie had heard that word used to describe cakes, frosting, or even peanut butter—but never language.

Mrs. Flaherty plopped into a chair and looked at the air above her forehead as if what she wanted to say was written in a cartoon bubble. "Over your years as a student, Jamie, perhaps you were rewarded for big words, long sentences, and thick essays or research papers. However, not many of your readers out there, including teachers, have the time to read such padded material. Rather than end up bored, frustrated, or tired, we push it aside or read it superficially at best -- especially if many of the words are mere fluff and lack any clear point."

Jamie could recall a few times when she had run out of things to write but the teacher had required a minimum number of pages for her paper. She remembered trying to add a paragraph here and there to meet the page requirement, but felt like she was forcing the words and they didn't really add anything to her writing.

"So, Jamie," Mrs. Flaherty said, "to combat wordiness, you must first recognize your 'fluff' and cut it out. You'll notice the handout gets at ways to attack fluff."

Jamie read aloud:

Attack the Fluff

The key way to attack fluff is to **guard against wordy sentences**. You can drown your ideas in too many words. Consider the student's sentence: *The Harlem Renaissance was a cultural revolution for all people, which emerged from the black culture which dominated the stage transcending it into the pulse of the people.*

"I'm not sure what this person is trying to say." Jamie looked up at her teacher. "Is the sentence too long?"

"Well, Mrs. Flaherty replied, "That's *one* big problem with it. It's about the length of an average sentence in academic, government, or business writing—maybe close to 30 words. If you look at one of your typed essays with 12-point font and one-inch margins, an average-length sentence is shorter. Just under 20 words or about one-and-a-half lines long. If most of your sentences are more than four or even five lines long, chances are your writing is too wordy and your readers are frustrated."

Jamie nodded. She had never thought about paying attention to the wordiness of her sentences.

"Besides looking at the actual length, there are other ways of telling when a sentence is too wordy and unclear. I wrote them down on the sheet in front of you, Jamie."

Jamie read:

A sentence is *too* wordy when
- **It loses your reader.**
- **It fails the short-term memory test—you, yourself, cannot recite it aloud or remember it without looking at your paper.**
- **It is peppered with too many punctuation marks. For example, it has four commas, one colon, two dashes, one semicolon, and**

quotation marks.

"Keep in mind, Jamie," Mrs. Flaherty broke in, "A long sentence here and there—as long as it is well written—is fine. But too many long sentences, and poorly written ones, are a problem. Variation is the key. By varying the length of your sentences, your writing, like music, takes on a tempo and rhythm all its own. The handout describes some simple strategies to vary the length of your sentences and paragraphs, and keep your writing clear, and fluff-free."

Jamie continued to read.

Attack the Fluff (cont.)

➡ **Vary the length of your sentences** to make your writing dynamic. Experiment with short sentences. Powerful ideas can be expressed in ten words or fewer. Strive for an average of about 18 words or sentences that are one-and-a-half typed lines long. Try to include one or two longer sentences that are at least 27 words or over two typed lines of your page, but make sure each sentence is limited to one clear idea and the details to support and describe it.

➡ **Avoid redundancies.** When revising your writing, watch for the use of the same word or phrase more than once within a sentence or paragraph—unless, of course, you are repeating yourself for purposes of style or transition. Needless repetition annoys the reader. Instead, eliminate altogether or paraphrase the redundant words or phrases. For example, if you were writing about a problem you experienced, using the word "problem" several times in a short, five-paragraph essay might frustrate your reader. You could rephrase "problem" as a challenge, dilemma, difficult situation, or use the transitional technique of repeating the phrase that describes the problem.

"I've got a great example of avoiding redundancies," Mrs. Flaherty said. "How many times do you hear a word or phrase repeated in this paragraph?" She read:

"As a senior, I discovered that the college application process was similar to a full-time job. It took me hours to sift through the requirements for each school and make a 'to-do' list of all the things I needed to get done by specific deadlines. Applying to college was hard, but finding the time to do my homework and have a life too was the biggest challenge of all."

"Hmm," Jamie said. "I didn't really hear any words repeated at all, even though the idea of the college application process came up more than once. The writer found different ways to get the idea across without having to say 'college application process' again and again." Jamie nodded, then continued to read:

 Use words that are genuine, rather than forced, contrived, too poetic, or 'flowery.' Imagine yourself presenting your idea/s aloud to your reader. What would you say to get your meaning across in the simplest, most convincing way? How would your words flow? Use the language you naturally speak as your guide.

For example, which of the following sentences "flows" more naturally?
"This militaristic family was perhaps most affected socially by the changes the war brought about." **Or,** *"The war affected this military family most in social ways."*
"When she first heard him she told none of this to anybody." **Or,** *"She didn't tell anybody what he had said."*

 Keep the subject and verb close together. The lengthier the sentence, the more this subject-verb link can be obscured. Trying to pack too many ideas between the subject and verb is risky. The reader may lose track of who or what is doing the action or what the action is. And if there's a direct object, the reader may lose track of who's receiving the action. Which one of the following sentences is clearer?

When the soldiers wearing disguises without a sound under the dark night sky attacked the ship, everyone was surprised.
Without a sound, the disguised soldiers attacked the ship under the dark night sky, surprising everyone.

 Limit each main idea to one sentence. And, limit each sentence to one main idea. A good strategy for writing clearly is to resist the urge to say too much in a sentence. Focus on one idea and one idea only.

For example, recall the wordy sentence:
"The Harlem Renaissance was a cultural revolution for all people, which emerged from the black culture which dominated the stage transcending it into the pulse of the people."
We could limit the sentence to one idea, and introduce it with a transition:
Although the Harlem Renaissance emerged from black culture, it was a cultural revolution for all people.
"Notice," Mrs. Flaherty added, "'transcending it into the pulse' is an example of unnecessary fluff, and we can omit it entirely here."
Jamie nodded and continued:

- **Use the active voice** (when the subject is actively doing something) as much as possible to draw your reader into the action of your argument.

    The Senator hand picked his legislative assistant. (Active Voice)
    The legislative assistant was hand picked by the Senator. (Passive Voice)

- **Write a "friendly"-looking essay.** Break down lengthy paragraphs (for the same reasons that we avoid too many lengthy sentences) by limiting each paragraph to one main idea and the supporting details. In short essays, vary the length of each paragraph to between three and seven sentences or between four and nine typed lines. If a paragraph extends well beyond ten lines and looks like a dense wall of words, it might scare off a few readers.

- **Capture your precise meaning.** Replace words that are general and vague (e.g., happy, great, bad, amazing, fabulous, good, a lot, wonderful, incredible, beautiful, horrible, etc.) with specific ones that reflect the subtle nuances of meaning (e.g., "The night was sultry" vs. "The night was hot.") Remember, the more precise your words and meaning, the more deeply the reader can engage in your unique voice and experience.

- **Avoid jargon or slang**—the specialized vocabulary you use in the school lunchroom with your friends. While you and your peers may understand it, the reader outside your circle of friends won't. Remember to use standard informal English—words that your readers are likely to be acquainted with.

- **Avoid phrases that state the obvious.** Without realizing it, we sometimes write what the reader already implicitly understands. For example, we might write needless phrases such as, *This essay is about...; This paragraph will focus on...; You will find it interesting to know...; This story is about...; It is obvious that...; It happened like this...; The purpose of this essay is to show that....*

Which of the following sentences is clearer?
"It's obvious in the novel <u>Native Son</u>, by Richard Wright, Bigger is a victim of growing up with the only knowledge of racism to guide him."
Or, "In Richard Wright's novel, <u>Native Son</u>, Bigger is a victim of racism..."

➤ **Cut out the repetition of ideas:** Often, we repeat what we have just said in subtle ways that can annoy and frustrate the reader. The following sentences would be more concise and convey the same meaning if the italicized phrases were removed:
The drinks range *in size* from small to very large.
The amount of the agreement was for $3,420.00.
It is possible that other reports might be based on outdated information.
Meetings were scheduled with each of the students *individually*.
The majority of the mistakes were primarily due to poor teamwork.

➤ **Drop meaningless prepositional phrases.** We frequently use wordy prepositional phrases when a simple, direct word would convey the meaning. Here are some common examples:
In view of the fact that [*because*]
with regard to [*regarding, about*]
in the event that [*if*]
in order to [*to*]
despite the fact that [*although, though*]
at the earliest date [*soon*]
at all times [*always*]
on the basis of [*by*]

➤ **Resist the overuse of big words (like those from your SAT vocabulary lists!)** Instead, rely on the use of simple but powerful language to convey a wide range of human experience. If you must use big words, use them sparingly and make sure that readers would be able to figure out their meaning from the context of your writing. In which of the following sentences is the meaning of the word *conundrum* clearer? *Allie was in a conundrum and wondered what to do next.*
Allie looked at the mess she had caused, wondering how she could get herself out of this conundrum.

➤ **At the beginning of each paragraph, brace your reader for what is to follow.** Have your topic sentence succinctly summarize the main idea of the paragraph. Just as a clear introduction sets the stage for the rest of your essay and enables your reader to more easily follow your argument, the first sentence of each paragraph prepares your reader for the next main idea or link in that argument.

Jamie looked up from her guidelines and student examples, relieved that she couldn't claim any sentences as her own. "Some of these sentences sound pretty muddled," she admitted to her teacher. "Amazing what cutting out the fluff will do."

"Between now and the SAT, Jamie, I want you to go over some of your essays and papers that you have already written and rewrite each wordy sentence using one of these techniques for avoiding fluff. And at least a couple of times before the big day, make up an SAT question, set your timer for 25 minutes, pretend you are in the room of the test, and write.

"Can you believe, Jamie," she continued, "the next time we meet, the SAT will be over? Of course, I'll be dying to hear how it went for you. And to hear what the SAT essay question is. Good luck, my dear!" The teacher gave Jamie a big hug.

Just like that, Jamie marveled. All the months of hard work and *poof*, just like that, it was over.

"Thank you. I'll be back!" Jamie warned. She couldn't think of any more words to thank her teacher. And somehow, she knew it didn't matter. She didn't need to add any fluff to her appreciation. Her eyes said enough.

As she turned to leave, Jamie turned her thoughts to the SAT essay and for the first time, she wasn't worried about what score she would get. Instead, she hoped that her essay would clearly communicate ideas to the rater who graded it. If she could touch a stranger with her writing, in her own authentic voice—no fluff!—that would be the best thanks of all.

— Epilogue —

Donna stared at the computer screen, struggling to click her mind into focus. She couldn't read the words. They looked like they were written in a foreign alphabet—ancient hieroglyphics, maybe. Nothing she could make sense of.

That morning, Donna had found Sara's pillow drenched in tears. Her three-year-old had sobbed off and on through the night, "Daddy, don't go 'way! Stay here, Daddy!" Although Donna had tried to comfort her, she knew that she couldn't provide what her daughter wanted the most. Rick was gone. The family they had known was split for good.

Donna replaced Sara's sheets, hoping that the soft, dry flannel patterned with dancing ponies would sooth her daughter's anguish. Within minutes, Sara was in a deep slumber, freeing Donna to work.

Donna had several SAT essays to rate by noon. Usually, she could get them done quickly. In a few weeks, she hoped to be promoted to supervisor—a role that paid more and gave her the opportunity to manage other raters.

But now, after the difficult night, she was fighting to rate just one essay. She blinked her eyes hard, willing her mind to focus once and for all. Finally, as if the words suddenly appeared out of a fog, Donna was able to read the first few sentences.

When my parents divorced, I felt like my whole life had fallen apart. So much of who I was had been shaped by my family —my mother, father, and John, my big brother. For fourteen years, I thought we were one tight, indestructible unit. We ate together, laughed and cried together, and often fought hard, but we were able to stay together. When my father moved into an apartment on the opposite side of town, I felt lost and betrayed. At least when we were fighting, the family was still under one roof. Now, the door had closed on my parents' marriage, forcing each of us to start over. We had to remake who we were without the traditional family unit to define us.

Donna was stunned. Could it be? Someone out there had been through what she and her daughter were now facing. The words, delivered through cyberspace, brought to life a perspective that maybe one day, both she and Sara could express. But today, the experience was still too new and painful.

Although the door had shut on their marriage, another door opened to some talents and opportunities my parents never knew they had. Before she separated from my father, my mother had trouble changing a light bulb. Now she started shopping at Home Depot, tearing down walls, and creating an airy kitchen out of the ruins of a cluttered closet. My father, who once claimed he would poison us all if forced to cook dinner, was—after some initial disasters—creating perfect honey wheat bread, cream of asparagus soup, and edible meat loaf.

Even though the words were funny, Donna found herself reaching for a tissue. "This kid is only in high school," she thought, dabbing her eyes, "but I feel like this essay is written for me."

John changed, too, after the break up. Although at first I was too busy feeling sorry for myself to even care about what my brother was going through, after a few months I noticed that he was taking out the garbage and recyclables without being asked. When he saw that I was upset over a fight I had had with a close friend, John asked if I wanted to go to the movies with him and his girlfriend. And when we had just one car to share between us, he always made sure to check with me before driving off. John started acting like he liked me. I was comforted knowing that even if my parents' relationship had crumbled, the ties I had with my brother would last.

As for me, well, let's just say my door was stuck. It was a while before I could open it a crack and start dealing with my own worst enemy -- my anger and self-doubts. In language arts that year, we had to read On Death and Dying, *by E. Kubler Ross. I couldn't believe how much divorce was like death. I went through the same stages of grief that people go through when they know they are going to die: shock, denial, anger, sadness, and finally, acceptance and moving on.*

Even through my shock and denial, I realized my teachers and counselors had some useful advice for me if I would only listen. They told me to channel my anger towards some constructive purpose—something I could do something about, like dropping time in swimming. Or helping my mother tear down the closet walls. They taught me that my sadness was a sign that I needed to go to people for support, not push my friends away. And over time, I accepted the fact that family doesn't have to be one cohesive unit. By dividing in one way, we end up multiplying in others—like a river that forks and courses on in new directions. Each time a door closes on how our family used to be, another door opens to the strengths and possibilities hidden inside us.

Resting her forehead on her palms, Donna finally let the tears flow. This time, she pushed away the tissues. Strangely, this cry was different. It wasn't choking, but freeing. Her chest felt lighter. A young writer had given her hope when she needed it the most.

Donna loved the images she took away from this essay. She imagined herself at a powerful fork in the river. Her family—like the one in the essay—had decided to branch in new directions, close the door on what wasn't working, and open another door to new possibilities. At the start of the essay, all she could see was the door that had closed.

Donna took a deep breath and reminded herself of the task at hand. She still had to assign the essay a score on a scale of one to six. Time to be objective. By now, she had committed the criteria for a high-scoring essay to memory. To achieve a "6," the College Board expected students to "effectively and insightfully develop a point of view on the issue, show outstanding critical thinking, using clearly appropriate examples, reasons, and other evidence to support their position. Their essays had to be well organized and clearly focused, demonstrating clear coherence and smooth progression of ideas. Students had to exhibit the skillful use of language, using a varied, accurate, and apt vocabulary and a meaningful variety in sentence structure. Their essays also had to be free of most errors in grammar, usage, and mechanics."

Mentally, Donna checked off each of the essay's strengths: Yes, it was well organized. The writer had presented introductory, body, and concluding paragraphs—each one devoted to the development of an idea that was central to the overall argument with at least three details to support it. The second paragraph, for example, addressed the positive changes that the brother, John, went through after his parents' divorce—supporting the writer's claim that when one door closes, a window opens to new strengths and possibilities. John became more helpful at home by taking out the garbage, and more considerate of his sibling by extending an invitation to the movies.

Donna also noted the range in vocabulary. The writer used both simple and more complex words, such as *tight* and *cohesive* to describe the family unit, and precise words such as *crumbled* to illustrate what had happened to the parents' relationship.

Donna also noticed that the sentences flowed smoothly from one to the next without the choppiness that was characteristic of many essays. This student used a variety of sentence structures to contribute to the flow of the writing, ranging from simple subject-verb constructions in the active voice, such as *I accepted the fact* to more intricate sentences beginning with transitional words and phrases, such as *although, when,* and *as for me.* The writer made sure to launch a new idea after connecting it to the last one with an appropriate transition.

Finally, Donna could tell this writer knew how to express his or her insights in a genuine voice by 1) critically reflecting on the divorce experience and telling the reader what s/he had learned from it, 2) using descriptive imagery to illustrate the experience, 3) displaying consistent facility in the use of language and transitions, and 4) writing clearly. This writer knew how to show and tell with heart in mind.

"You deserve a good grade for your insights alone," Donna thought, "And your ability to touch others with the lessons you have learned from your experience." Her cheeks were still damp with tears. "I'm convinced. When one door closes, another door opens. If we only look to find it. Insight," If we only look to find it. Insight," she recalled from her scoring rubric, "is the mark of a high-scoring essay."

Donna looked at the name on the essay. "Hmm. Jamie. Could be a boy or girl. Whoever you are, thank you and good luck," she wished the young writer. Then, clicking inside the box by 6, she pressed submit and cleared the screen for a new essay.

Bibliography

Atkinson, Richard C., "Standardized Tests and Access to American Universities," 2001 Robert Atwell Distinguished Lecture, 83rd Annual Meeting of the American Council on Education, Washington, D.C., February 18, 2001 (see http://www.ucop.edu/pres/prespeeches.html).

Csikszentmihalyi, M. (1988). Optimal experience: Psychological studies of flow in consciousness. Cambridge, NY: Cambridge University Press.

Csikszentmihalyi, M. (1991). Flow: The psychology of optimal experience. New York:
Harper & Row.

Flower, Linda; Hayes, John R. (1981). A cognitive process theory of writing. College Composition and Communication, Vol. 32, No. 4, 365-87.

Hayakawa, S.I. (1939). Language in thought and action. (Enlarged ed.). San Diego: Harcourt Brace Jovanovich, 1978.

Kolb, D. A. (1984). Experiential Learning: Experience as the source of learning and development. Englewood Cliffs, N. J.: Prentice-Hall.

Kolb. D. A., & Fry, R. (1975). Toward an applied theory of experiential learning. In C. Cooper (ed.). Theories of Group Process, London: John Wiley.

Perry, Susan K. (1999). Writing in flow: Keys to enhanced creativity. Cincinnati: Writer's Digest Books.

Stein, C. (1990). Stein's clenched fist technique. In Hammond, D. Corydon, (Ed.), Handbook of hypnotic suggestions and metaphors, (pp.145-147). New York, London: W. W. Norton & Company.

Townsend, Michael A. R., Hicks, Lynley, Thompson, Jacquilyn D. M., Wilton, Keri M., Tuck, Bryan F., & Moore, Dennis W. (1993). Effects of introductions and conclusions in assessment of student essays. Journal of Educational Psychology, December, Vol. 85, No. 4, 670–678.